*"It is the prayer and song of ou[...]
us on fire with Himself and fo[...]
presence and surrender our liv[...]
mission. Malcolm Macdonald [...]
costly transformation the fire of God brings."*
                    – Mark Bailey, National Leader, New Wine

*"This book is a virtual incendiary device designed to ignite
the heart of every reader. It pulsates with passion and a
longing for an authentic encounter with the living God. Such
encounters are transformational. Today's persecuted church
knows all about this. The holy fire that has consumed them
consumed the early church also. I'm left praying the prayer: O
Lord, for Your glory set me on fire today!"*
                    – Eddie Lyle, President, Open Doors UK

*"The title of this book is a bold prayer, but one that is
embodied in Malcolm Macdonald's own life and ministry.
This is a book that speaks out of deep personal experience, the
wisdom of years of ministry, and a burning desire for God and
His presence."*
                – Rt Revd Dr Graham Tomlin, Bishop of Kensington

*"As children we were taught not to go too near the fire or we
would be burned. The Christian life teaches something else.
Another fire. One that burns brightly, but does not consume.
We don't just need to go near it. We must receive it. This
happened to Moses, and his life was changed. It happened to
Mary, and the Christ was born. It happened to the apostles,
and the church grew. That same fire is available today. So read
this book carefully: it will burn you."*
                – Rt Revd Stephen Cottrell, Bishop of Chelmsford

"I have found this to be a very refreshing, deeply challenging, extremely honest, and very readable book. It hits right at the heart of the need of Western Christianity and in particular the individual Christian's need to know the full and sanctifying power of the Holy Spirit. It is a clear call to wholly follow the Lord no matter what the apparent cost. The passion and openness with which the author shares transform the book from being a mere doctrinal thesis into a genuine heartfelt cry for the spiritual climate of our nation to be transformed by a church genuinely set on fire by God. May He answer prayer!"
— **John Townend**, General Director, The Faith Mission

"Revival seems to be on many people's lips as they see the move of the Spirit and the need of the world; our histories contain many stories of God's supernatural intervention changing communities and nations in incredible ways; and the Scriptures themselves are filled with promises of which we know we've only seen the smallest fulfilment in our days. Yet often these appear to be completely different things. This book brings them together in a way that will expand your vision and ignite your faith. Read it carefully and prayerfully, and you may never be the same again."
— **Revd Paul Harcourt**, Regional Director, London and East, New Wine

"Malcolm is a man who writes about fire with fire. He is a leader in the land with a vital message for today's church. I loved the section on the fire of suffering. This book fed me and stirred me to come back to my first love. Read it slowly, prayerfully, and with longing. May this book help to bring us into the season of revival we all long for."
— **Revd Charlie Cleverly**, St Aldates Oxford

Set Me on Fire

Being filled with the presence of God

Malcolm Macdonald

MONARCH
BOOKS

Oxford UK, and Grand Rapids, USA

Published by Monarch Books
an imprint of
Lion Hudson plc
Wilkinson House, Jordan Hill Road,
Oxford OX2 8DR, England
Email: monarch@lionhudson.com
www.lionhudson.com/monarch

ISBN 978 0 85721 691 5
e-ISBN 978 0 85721 692 2

First edition 2015

Acknowledgments
Unless otherwise indicated Scripture quotations are taken from the Holy
Bible, New International Version Anglicised. Copyright © 1979, 1984,
2011 Biblica, formerly International Bible Society. Used by permission of
Hodder & Stoughton Ltd, an Hachette UK company. All rights reserved.
"NIV" is a registered trademark of Biblica. UK trademark number
1448790.
Scripture quotations marked "NKJV" taken from the New King James
Version. Copyright © 1982 by Thomas Nelson, Inc. Used by permission.
All right reserved.

A catalogue record for this book is available from the British Library

Printed and bound in Great Britain by Clays Ltd, St Ives plc

I dedicate this book to my beautiful wife Caroline
and my beloved children: Beth, Lucy and Joshua.
May we ever grow as a family on fire for God.

Contents

Foreword

A few years ago I set off as usual on a Sunday morning to speak at a church. On this occasion I was headed for Loughton, Essex, and on arrival met the new vicar. Initially I thought him to be a mild-mannered man but in truth he was one full of the Spirit, ambitious in vision and fired up for Jesus. The vicar was the author of this book, Malcolm Macdonald. In the years that have passed I have enjoyed getting to know him more and am proud to call him my friend.

This wonderful book is his manifesto to the church. It's practical, powerful, and inspiring. If read at face value it should come with a health warning because if taken seriously the words inside it will change your own life, that of your church, and that of your community forever. I find myself sharing Malcolm's longing for a mighty move of God that would transform this nation, for the God of the miraculous to do what seems impossible and turn this land around. Enough of decline, apathy, and pessimism; I wholeheartedly concur with Malcolm's belief that things can be different. I love the idea of this and share his heart for a renewed landscape fuelled by a fired-up church.

His cry for us as a church to awaken is deeply challenging. In truth, this book often makes for uncomfortable reading, but in a good way. Even if you don't agree with every word, you can't help but be challenged by the call to see greater spiritual power in our churches, which all starts with a stronger belief in the power of the Holy Spirit.

Malcolm grapples with Scripture beautifully and cites numerous examples from church history too. The book flows wonderfully and it's really hard to put down. At the same time he doesn't hide away from difficult issues such as the spiritual battle that is taking place, the reality of our sin, and the inherent need to pursue holiness.

In essence, the challenge of this book is to pursue greater fire in our encounters with God, to have a deeper and stronger experience of Him, to be filled further and continually by the Spirit, and to pursue greater intimacy with Him. This challenge is for us individually and the church corporately in order that the nation would be changed.

As a result of reading this book I find myself personally wanting to pursue even greater intimacy with God and looking to give my life yet further in complete surrender. My prayer is that, as Malcolm warns us, my fears won't stop me doing this wholeheartedly. The pages of this book resonate with me massively as they talk about the kind of "on-fire" and dangerous Christianity that I want to be a part of. Like Malcolm, I long to see this nation turned inside out, upside down, and back to front for Christ. I believe we will see a major revival in our time, but to start with let's have a deeper encounter with Him.

I thank God that Malcolm has written this. It's a book for our time. So strap yourself in and enjoy the adventure that lies ahead on these pages. Ask the Lord to set you on fire for Him. It just might change everything!

Gavin Calver
Director of Mission, Evangelical Alliance

Acknowledgments

This book comes from my heart. It is not so much a systematic study of the fire of God as a sincere prayer that has been in my heart for many years. It was written at the time of a sabbatical during which God graciously showed me so much about my church, my family, myself, and Himself.

I want to thank my amazing church family of St Mary's Loughton, for their love, support, and encouragement over the past six years. I have learned so much from them. I believe we need to put what is written here into practice in the local church and with our family and friends. So thank you to my family and friends at St Mary's for journeying with me in all this.

I also want to acknowledge the role of New Wine in helping this book come into being. The core of the book was first taught at a series of early morning seminars at New Wine in 2011, where hundreds turned out to hear about the fire of God. God moved during those times in His power, and that was when I sensed His touch on this material. I am grateful for the vision and ministry of New Wine and am glad to be part of that movement to see local churches change nations.

Introduction

Be who God meant you to be and you will set the world on fire.
St Catherine of Siena

We know instinctively that we are called to be a fiery church. We sing about God's consuming fire in our worship and know that this is more than mere sentiment. It is about a deeper and life-changing encounter with God. Somehow, we know we were made for more. We are meant to be fiery disciples. I believe there is a profound longing today for the fire of God to set us on fire so that we would be who God always meant us to be.

The Bible is full of fire from Genesis to Revelation. Fire is at the heart of many themes of Scripture. Fire carried God's intimate presence and also His most terrible judgments. Fire manifested God's breathtaking power through Elijah on Mount Carmel and His awesome holiness at the dedication of Solomon's temple. Fire devoured Sodom and Gomorrah and yet protected and guided the Hebrews for forty years in the wilderness. The Old Testament contains a great deal of fire.

The New Testament picks up the theme very quickly and quite differently with John the Baptist announcing that Jesus would baptize with the Holy Spirit and with fire. Sure enough, fire marked the coming of the Holy Spirit at Pentecost. From that moment fire became a clear symbol of the Spirit-filled life. The New Testament ends with fiery images of God's throne and descriptions of fire in both heaven and hell. It is no surprise that scenes of the return of Jesus are set against a backdrop of fire. Remarkably, even Jesus' eyes are described as "blazing fire" in Revelation 1:14.

Where does all this leave us? Fire is indispensable in the Christian life. There is no healthy Christian life without fire. God's fire represents His character. Our God is white-hot with love, holiness, power, light, and glory. The hunger to be "set on fire for God" longs for an undiluted, bright, powerful, and beautiful reflection of God through our lives. That is why fire goes to the heart of Christian discipleship and experience.

This book comes from a deep place of personal longing in my own life. I want to be set on fire for God in my generation. I want to burn for God and I want my church family and whole community to feel the power of His divine fire. I have read so many accounts of revival that I feel have ruined me for the ordinary. Who wants church to be average? Why be spiritually tepid? Who actually believes in being mediocre?

Why does the Bible use the language of fire? I believe that earthly images are often a small reflection of a great eternal truth. The Bible uses fire, water, oil, and wind as pictures to help us experience spiritual truths. They have all been used in Scripture to refer to the person and ministry of the Holy Spirit. The Spirit is so wonderful, and God wants us to understand how He works in us. I love the simple way the Bible picks up the theme of fire as shorthand to capture how God moves. Fire spreads rapidly. It is powerful, it destroys impurities, it releases light and power, and it is a symbol of passion. Fire is part of our everyday experience. We can't live without it. What a fascinating visible emblem of God's character and symbol of His work in us. As Luke 24:32 records, God wants our hearts to burn within us as we encounter Him.

Are We Ready for Fire?

The idea of being "on fire" as a Christian is exhilarating, but let's be honest, it can also feel quite overwhelming. If you are like me, you might sometimes feel perplexed about what it really means to be on fire for God. It can also seem like an unattainable ideal. Will I be able to keep it up for more than two weeks? How will it affect everyday life? What about my family and other people close to me? Being set on fire is God's will for us, but how do we get there? It has to mean something distinctive. It has to mean something in private as well as in public. What could it actually look like for me to be on fire for God?

I wonder if we have bought into a rose-tinted and distorted sense of what it looks like to be on fire for God. It has to be more than a mere short-term special spiritual effort. It is much more transforming, costly, and life-altering. As I read the Bible, it seems to me that being on fire means being filled, possessed, and saturated with God. It means having a God-filled personality. It is about full surrender and loving devotion. It is about obedience no matter what it costs. There is something genuinely supernatural being worked out in ordinary and everyday life here. This means that we can still work, rest, play, share faith, share the gospel, teach, pray, serve, enjoy family, laugh, and cry so long as He is Lord and our First Love. Being on fire is not about being over-intense or super-spiritual; it is about genuine surrender rooted in worship and adoration.

So how about it? Are we ready for the fire of God? If I am very honest, I feel that much contemporary church experience is too focused on treating Christians as fickle consumers rather than fiery disciples. Is our faith on fire from Monday to Saturday as well as on Sunday? Our consumer-culture version of Jesus seems quite content to bless, rather than challenge, our choices and lifestyles. Is this the same Jesus we read about in the gospels? I recently read through the whole New Testament in bigger chunks that I have ever read before. Something that struck me powerfully is how costly living out the Christian faith really is. In Britain, we spend our lives seeking safety, ease, and comfort. Yet the church I read about in the New Testament ran towards sacrifice, servanthood, and risk. What is our goal in life: getting our needs met, or laying our lives down?

We have somehow squared a circle that allows us to avoid any sacrifice that seems a bit too extreme or costly. Some Christians can't even commit to regularly gathering for worship with the church family more than once every few weeks. This has become the new normal in churches. We now accept the growing church culture of struggling to fit in coming together to worship Almighty God. Some go to church as long as they don't have anything better planned. Church has become part of our spectrum of consumer choices in life, with ourselves at the centre. Does God have any "off limits" areas in your life? Do we think Jesus minds how we live? Would He applaud our self-sufficiency? Would Jesus commend or challenge our mindsets and lifestyles?

The issue of commitment in the British church is huge. Many have lost the connection with covenant relationships, sacrifice, servanthood, and dying to self. We are in danger of making up our own version of Christianity in our own image. It is hard for the self-centred to enter the kingdom of heaven. God's kingdom turns the values and culture of the world upside down. We have lost much of the sense of what it means to be radical and so we don't seem to expect too much fire. Where has all the fire gone?

Being on fire for God will cost us everything. There is always a cost in true discipleship. We must die to reputation, sinful habits, attitudes, strongholds, and mediocrity. Dying to sin means we are truly free to live for Christ in the power of His resurrection. The way to freedom is a fiery path of surrender, brokenness, humility, and even persecution. Are we ready to go through with God no matter what it costs? Are we ready for the fire? Do we know what we are asking for when we seek the fire of God in our lives, churches, and nation? We had better count the cost and go through with it, rather than start out only to back off later.

As I write, I feel challenged to the core about my own life. For me, writing this book is like praying a heartfelt prayer. As I read my Bible, I can honestly say that I know full well I have no power in myself to live for Christ. Without Him I can do nothing. Do we believe that? I am desperately in need of the Holy Spirit – and so are you. I want the fire I see in the Bible and through church history, which ignited God's people, to display His power and love. I want that in my town and in my generation. Don't you? I want to see the difference the fire of God makes in lives. I want to find out what it means to be on fire for God in the face of our consumer culture. The fire will change everything. Are we ready for that?

Our world needs a demonstration of a church set on fire with the love of Jesus Christ. This book will try to explain what that fire means. What would it look like in our churches? Fire is not safe; it spreads rapidly. It can destroy or create. It is a powerful force in both the natural and the spiritual realms. I understand that being on fire for God can seem an unfamiliar, even old-fashioned concept. We will try to explore it together, but can I also ask you to pray as you read this book, for a vision of what your life would be like with the fire of God burning in your heart?

This fire will birth a vision for revival, growth, and freedom. It will take you to a place of encounter, intimacy, love, and purity. The fire is for broken people. It is for people who feel they have failed and are at the end of themselves. The fire comes to anyone who knows they need God. God is so close to people who are hungry and dependent on Him. There is such transformation in that place.

The essence of this book is a call, a challenge, and an invitation to experience God's fiery character and heart. Do you long for a nation-changing move of God in our generation? I dream about seeing God glorified in my own town, in the UK, and around the world. I don't have all the answers, but I know I long to see the church ablaze and bright with Jesus. As you read, remember that for me, this is more like writing a prayer than a book, so please read and pray along with me: "O Lord, for Your glory, set me on fire today."

Chapter 1

God's Fiery Presence

As we rejoice in the gift of this new day, so may the light of
your Presence, O God, set our hearts on fire with love for you;
now and for ever.[1]

Common Worship, Morning Prayer

Encountering God's Presence

I love the presence of God. How could we ever adequately
express the beauty, power, and reality of the glorious presence
of God? For me, there is nothing to compare to the awareness
of His nearness. We have nothing better to do in this life than
be in His presence. Beholding God with the eyes of our heart,
we find Him more glorious in holiness and love than we had
imagined. We can cultivate a depth of relationship with God
that goes far beyond an hour on a Sunday. You can never be
the same after encountering God. We must never settle for
half-hearted and jaded religion that has to be endured, not
enjoyed. God wants us to know Him. It really matters that
every Christian cultivates a lifestyle of encounter with God.
Seeking His presence is the only way to sustain a fire-filled
Christian life. Encountering God changes everything.

1 *Common Worship*, London: Church House Publishing, 2000,
p. 32.

What do I mean by "encounter"? In my experience, it is about heart-to-heart personal connection with God. It is moving from knowing about God to being transformed by being with Him. Encounter is about actually having a relationship with God that takes me over. God has captured my heart and my life is now His. At its heart is the experience of His goodness. It is tasting and seeing God as He is, and allowing the atmosphere of His eternal beauty and glory to pervade our lives. When this happens, there is a great intimacy as well as an awesome holy fear. Encounter is not centred on my needs and me; it is about God. It is birthed in the place where we see God for who He is. Seeing God, as He is, even just a glimpse of Him, will leave us breathless with holy fear, lost in wonder, and satiated with a closeness and intimacy we never thought possible. This kind of encounter means we will never thirst again.

Have you ever been completely overwhelmed by seeing God for who He really is? I will never forget the first time I read A. W. Tozer's book, *The Knowledge of the Holy*. The affection, awe, and friendship with God, with which Tozer described the attributes of God, drew me into God's presence in a whole new way. God is absolutely holy, perfect love, and outrageously good at the same time as revealing holy wrath as judge. He is able to be all this perfectly and simultaneously because He is perfect in holiness and love. I am completely astonished by who God is.

Another leader from whom I have learned much about God's presence is Mike Bickle. When I was a young adult, his beautiful book *Passion for Jesus* changed my life. I realized for the first time the tremendous affection Jesus has for me, and all I wanted to do was respond with abandonment to Him.

These spiritual fathers are friends of God. They know the value of the presence of God and they consider it nothing to give all to have that treasure. How hungry are we to be such friends of God? Are we ready for the fire to take hold of us?

The Bible is a catalogue of God encounters. They are rarer in the Old Testament as the Holy Spirit came upon particular people for specific tasks, but in the New Testament, the door is thrown wide open to everyone to encounter God. That is the heart of the gospel. God has always longed for His presence to be the priority of His people. Encountering God is a personal experience that changes your life. You can never be the same again.

Let me say very clearly that authentic God encounters start at the cross and the empty tomb of Jesus. They start as we bow our knee, confess our sin, believe in Jesus, and receive His gift of salvation. Jesus opened up the way to know God. He died and rose again to bring us to God, to make relationship with God possible. He rose again to bring us into the new life of the kingdom. Our relationship with God is dynamic because He is alive and we live with Him.

To encounter Him is also to be touched by His awesome fiery presence. Somehow, this fire expresses God's divine character. It is the fire *of God*. His fire captures His heart and the essence of His nature and character. That is why God wants a fiery church to represent Him. You can't meet with Him and be left cold and distant from Him. Fire is not merely the symbol of fervent faith; it goes to the heart of who God is and how He has chosen to reveal Himself to us. God is trying to communicate to us His priorities for our lives.

Divine fire is imparted through encounter. There are no shortcuts. A burning heart is ignited by an encounter. You will catch the fire from our fiery Father in heaven. There is so much more. We can have such a low expectation of the Christian life, but there is so much more than we have known. There is more of God than we know, but it comes through giving ourselves to Him more and more.

I meet so many people who feel a painful nagging sense of unworthiness or insignificance. They believe that Bible characters had God encounters, but they don't see that such encounters are available to them today. The devil does not mind you believing in the importance of meeting with God, as long as he can keep you from actually having an encounter yourself. This is more than good doctrine; it is rooted in holy and radical experience. What is keeping you from being set on fire through an encounter with God?

Face to Face with Fire

The Lord spoke to you face to face out of the fire on the mountain.

Deuteronomy 5:4

Moses was well acquainted with the fire of God and meeting with God, but the people were far more hesitant. For Moses, having face-to-face times with God was a necessity, not a luxury. Moses needed God's presence. He wholly depended upon it. We know that the presence of God was a big deal for Moses, who refused to go anywhere without the assurance of God's presence (Exodus 33:15).

The Ten Commandments were given to Moses against the backdrop of a fiery encounter. God wanted His people to be a people who encountered Him, but only Moses entered that blessing. The people held back because of fear. How they missed out! They could have known God as a whole nation in such a powerful way, yet they chose rather to stay distant and so ended up with a distorted view of Him. They could only see God through a lens of fear rather than with reverent intimacy. Understanding of who God is will affect what we believe we can experience of Him. That is why waiting upon God for who He is, is the key to encountering Him in prayer. Knowing God starts with seeing Him accurately by faith. Remember, the blessing for the pure in heart is to see God.

God's fire is for meant for you and me. We are meant to taste and feel its effect. Look at Joel 2:28 and Acts 2:17: God promised to pour out His Spirit on all people. Pentecost was an encounter. It made the presence of God available to everyone who believes. We need people today in our generation who have been to the fiery mountain of encounter with God and have heard His voice. In the place of encounter, that which is eternal becomes internal.

We can live from an encounter with God, and we can lead others into an encounter with Him. You and I are today as close to God as we actually want to be. What aspect of His fire does God want to pour into your life? It may be an increase of His holiness or intimacy and passion. Don't miss what God is doing in you, and don't be content to stay at a distance from Him.

My Meetings with God

Reflect with me for a while on your own experience of God. How would you describe your experience of His presence? There is a beautiful phrase in the first verse of Psalm 40: "I waited patiently for the Lord." I believe that this waiting upon God is the secret to our own encounters. We are so busy and task-focused in our lives, and this stressed-out way of living has affected our connection with God. Being willing to simply wait is vital. I don't mind how you wait, whether quietly or noisily, but we must wait. We are waiting upon Him. I love the simplicity of the prayer, "Come, Holy Spirit." Wait expectantly with this prayer on your heart and lips.

Before the outpouring of Pentecost, what were the followers of Jesus doing? Acts 1:4 holds a key for us: "Wait for the gift my Father promised." There is much emphasis today on simply receiving the Spirit through prayer ministry, and rightly so, but I would love to see us wait more upon God. There is a difference. Many people are not prepared to wait beyond five minutes, so the spark does not have time to burst into a flame. There is a heart preparation for the fire that can only be done in the time of waiting.

As I have reflected and remembered what God has been doing in my life over the past thirty years, some of the most significant moments were powerful encounters with God when I was on my knees by my bedside as a teenager. These precious moments with God still affect me to this day. It was here I learned to wait upon God. I became a Christian as a nine-year-old through a Faith Mission evangelist, Revd Angus Morrison, who came to our remote Hebridean island of Gigha in 1985. That was only the start of my journey in God's presence.

Although I attended church, I sadly wavered in my faith as I grew up. However, in 1991 I went to a Faith Mission conference in Bangor, Northern Ireland, and listened to a powerful South African preacher, Revd Roger Voke. I was deeply moved by the message of holiness, cleansing, and being filled with the Holy Spirit. I sat there gripped by God, with my heart thumping. I was desperate for God. I could hear Him calling me so gently and clearly. I knew I had been defeated by sin, double standards, and failure, and yet I knew God was speaking to me because He loved me. I felt broken-hearted over my condition and was aware of a heavy sense of God's presence as I went forward and responded to the call for prayer. All I can remember was the awesome and beautiful sense of His presence. The Holy Spirit was drawing me to Jesus, my First Love. That day, I came into an encounter with God from which I have never been the same and never want to recover.

I was often on my knees in my room after I was first filled with the Spirit. I had a map of the UK and I would spend time praying and weeping over the nation. During those early times with God, a seed of prayer and worship was planted in my heart that remains today. It was put there through an encounter with God's Father heart of love. I can remember times as a teenager when just opening my Bible caused tears to flow because God's love and the beauty of His glorious Word overwhelmed me. This is living from encounter with God. It brings a constant thankfulness and overwhelming sense of His goodness.

God did a powerful work of cleansing and empowering in my life. Over the next few years I discovered a new intimacy in worship and freedom in prayer that I had not known before. I spoke much more openly about Jesus to others. I was not ashamed of Jesus. I began to read about revival and listened to Duncan Campbell teaching about the revival on the Isle of Lewis. This made a deep impression on me as I began to hunger for the kinds of encounters that were frequent in revival but were not happening in my own life or church. I began to see that there was much more I knew nothing about, and I wanted to go deeper.

While at university in St Andrews, this passion grew and grew. Prayer, sharing my faith, and spending time in the Bible was a delight, not a duty. The times of greatest growth in my life have been because of an increase of the presence of God. My spiritual hunger and desire to live in the awareness of His presence meant that I felt overwhelmed by love. I did not care what others thought of me; I just wanted more of Him. We need these encounters. They remind us of who God is and who we are in Him. Fresh and clear meetings with God ignite passion, revive faith, and lead us more into love.

I am unapologetic about putting an emphasis on encountering and experiencing God's presence. We certainly need solid teaching and biblical understanding, but I believe that the purpose of the Bible is also to ignite holy fire in our hearts and for us to come into an intensely intimate relationship with God. We proclaim a gospel of relationship with God and invite people to come to Christ to begin that relationship, and then so often we lose focus on what that continuing and maturing relationship actually looks, sounds, and feels like.

The heart of encounter is to know Christ. Only God Himself can set you ablaze. It is not the worship, preaching, or ministry of a church that can transform us. There is no scarcity of good teaching today. Yet so many Christians are not on fire. Why? Perhaps even though we may attend a good church, we have not yet met with God Himself. I believe this is why so many churches and ministries struggle. There is a lack of a genuine encounter with God that wholly changes us from the inside out. At the heart of the story of every leader of revival you will find a life-changing encounter with God. Read the stories of men such as John Wesley, Jonathan Edwards, and Charles Finney. All of them testify to a powerful experience of God's Spirit that changed their lives before the revivals began. Our nation needs Jesus Christ, but He can only be truly represented by a church on fire, otherwise people are going to get a different gospel and a distorted Jesus. The stakes are high. The world waits for the church to catch fire.

Those early encounters were my first taste of the "much more" of God. I am still on the journey and still desperately need those fresh encounters as I move on with Him. I have tasted and seen and continue to long for more. Sometimes I have got down on my knees or prostrate on my face and wept in His presence; at other times I have danced or shouted with joy. I have sat quietly and listened, and at other times I have paced the floor in earnest prayer. But always the longing is for His presence. It is about Him, not us. It is time to wait, worship, pray, seek, hunger, and thirst – we need to encounter God Himself. Our God is the God who speaks face to face from the fire of His presence. Let's meet on the fiery mountain of encounter.

Marked by the Presence

My desire is to live a life marked by His presence. In Acts 4:13 there is a remarkable testimony: "When they saw the courage of Peter and John and realized that they were unschooled, ordinary men, they were astonished and they took note that these men had been with Jesus." Peter and John were marked by the presence of Jesus. They were ordinary men who were marked by God. How can we display that same testimony today?

How can we position ourselves to experience and encounter His presence so we can be marked by His presence?

Ask God to increase your hunger for Him

In all our longing and desire, sometimes we simply forget to ask. Spiritual hunger is so precious to God. Hunger means you will pay any price for the blessing of God Himself. Hunger does not settle for a half measure. Don't be afraid of spiritual hunger. King David was a man who hungered for God and was a man after God's heart. You could make one of his prayers your own. Pray Psalm 63 as you ask for an increase in hunger.

Turn your affections towards God in worship and adoration

Again, the psalms are a fertile place to go to find prayers of worship and adoration that lead to encounter with God. God is worthy of worship and praise. The Holy Spirit is drawn to worship. He is attracted to anyone giving God glory, thanks, and praise. Sing to the Lord, worship Him in the beauty of His holiness, and you will increase His presence in your life. Turning your affections means a constant posture of love towards God in your heart. Spend each day uttering expressions of adoring worship: "I love you, Jesus"; "Let Your name be glorified in me"; "Jesus, You are so worthy and I love you."

For me, this revelation of the Father's love and then going deeper in expressing love back to Him is at the heart of everything we are aiming for in the Christian life. Love is the centre. It is the greatest commandment and the essence of the Great Commission. Being undone by really experiencing and knowing the love of the Father, Son, and Holy Spirit is at the root of every divine encounter. There is nothing worth more than this, and in the light of this love no sacrifice is ever wasted. Knowing that God really loves me and delights in me, expressing love for Him in worship, and giving His love to others is essential. It is what being on fire for God is all about.

Repent of anything sinful or doubtful, and forgive everyone

The keys to receiving anything in the kingdom are repentance and faith. This was Jesus' first message: "Repent and believe the good news!" (Mark 1:15). Simply ask God to search your heart for anything that might grieve Him and then repent and turn to Him, making sure you follow through with any practical repentance required. This was a major emphasis of the Welsh preacher Evan Roberts in the revival of 1904.

I have often witnessed remarkable breakthroughs of freedom in people who have simply forgiven from the heart. Forgiveness is incredibly powerful. If you forgive others, God will forgive you (Matthew 6:14–15). Something I have found very powerful, yet very simple, has been to sit with a pen and paper and ask, "Father, please show me who I need to forgive." Then listen, write down names that come to mind, and take the time to forgive each one. Personally, I think in the light of Matthew 6:15, we can't afford not to forgive everyone. Some people see themselves as spiritually mature, yet cannot forgive. This can be difficult and can take time, but it is worth it.

Get onto your knees and pray out loud asking God to meet with you

I learned this as a teenager. There is something about being willing to bow down in prayer before the God of heaven and earth. We don't get on our knees very often – why not? It is good for us. Brother Yun recently preached in our church and spent the response time on his knees as he prayed for people. It was such an example of humility and a reminder of the Lordship of Jesus.

I strongly recommend praying out loud. This not only helps overcome distractions, but it also employs the power of the tongue. The Bible speaks of the power of our speech to bless and to curse (Proverbs 18:21). So let's practise the discipline of speaking out blessing in prayer. There is power in speaking out our prayers.

I would also encourage you to pray the Lord's Prayer. This prayer of Jesus is a trusted avenue into God's presence. Pray it through line by line and linger on each phrase as God leads you.

Read Scripture expecting to hear God speak to you

We are to be people of both Word and Spirit. Read the Bible with the aim of knowing God and hearing His voice. God loves to speak through His Word. Jesus loved the Scriptures and they were constantly on His lips. Let's love the Word and find Christ in every line. Don't neglect the Bible. Everything God does has its roots in Scripture. The Bible is God-breathed and you will hear His voice and meet Him face to face in the fire of the Word. You can only maintain spiritual fire by loving the Word.

Wait – don't rush God, and be willing to give time to prayer

This is about relationship, and it takes time. Someone said you can grow a mushroom in six hours, but it takes sixty years to grow an oak tree. Be ready for this to take time. Sometimes you will just sit quietly with God. Don't be anxious about it. God can see you. He loves you and will come to you. Remember Psalm 40:1 calls us to wait upon God, never giving up. Persevere in praying, "Come, Holy Spirit." How do we know how long to wait? We wait until He comes. You will know.

Share your faith with others and speak of Jesus openly

This comes straight from my own experience. I have found that if I have not recently shared my faith then I can become dulled and flat in my relationship with God. When I share Jesus with others, I find that I am much closer to Him. This also applies to serving people. I love finding God's presence in serving others. He will reveal Himself in acts of love and as we take risks in sharing our faith. Try it and see for yourself.

Declare the truth and promises of God over your life

I have begun doing this more recently. We all listen far too much to the lies of the devil about us. He is the father of lies and our accuser. One great way to break free from the lies is to openly declare the truth of the promises of God. This was what Jesus did when He defeated the devil in the wilderness. He declared the Word and won the battle. Ask God to show you

His promises. For example, "Father, I declare with thankfulness that You are my provider and You will supply every need." This is rooted in Philippians 4:19. Declarations must be rooted in God's promises found in Scripture, not merely in my imagination. The Bible is packed full of declarations that can strengthen our faith. We are called to speak life.

Obey the Holy Spirit's promptings

Mary's advice to the servants at the wedding at Cana was, "Do whatever he tells you" (John 2:5). Acts 5:32 reminds us that the Spirit is given to those who obey. It's pretty simple really: God wants us to hear and obey Him. The key for us is to remember His goodness in our obedience. He knows what is best for us.

Is there any area in which we are delaying obedience or where we are disobeying God? Are you ready to listen and obey in everyday life and allow God to make something ordinary into something holy?

Count the cost; then say "Yes!"

Encountering God will change you, but there is a choice to make. It cost Jesus everything to open your way to the Father. He chose to lay down His life for us. Take seriously the call of Christ upon your life. It is a call to discipleship, and it is a choice of your will to say "Yes". Count the cost, but when doing so, remember the words of Paul in Philippians 3:7–14:

But whatever were gains to me I now consider loss for the sake of Christ. What is more, I consider everything a loss because of the surpassing worth of knowing Christ Jesus my Lord, for whose sake I have lost all things. I consider them garbage, that I may gain Christ and be found in him, not having a righteousness of my own that comes from the law, but that which is through faith in Christ – the righteousness that comes from God on the basis of faith. I want to know Christ – yes, to know the power of his resurrection and participation in his sufferings, becoming like him in his death, and so, somehow, attaining to the resurrection from the dead.

Not that I have already obtained all this, or have already arrived at my goal, but I press on to take hold of that for which Christ Jesus took hold of me. Brothers and sisters, I do not consider myself yet to have taken hold of it. But one thing I do: forgetting what is behind and straining towards what is ahead, I press on towards the goal to win the prize for which God has called me heavenwards in Christ Jesus.

I believe the time has come for the church in the UK to be marked by the presence of God. We need an increase of His presence. There is a hunger to turn to the Lord and to encounter Him in a much deeper way that releases a greater maturity, faithfulness, and love in the church. We are hungry for His presence. There must be more.

Chapter 2

Consumed with Holy Fire

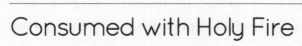

For the Lord your God is a consuming fire, a jealous God.
Deuteronomy 4:24

Our God is a consuming fire.
Hebrews 12:29

God is Radically Holy

The fire of God burns fiercely with holy purity. Holiness is God's pure life and light in us. It is His perspective revealed in us, His character displayed through us, and His wisdom flowing through us. A person or church on fire for God is consumed with holy love.

I strongly believe in the spiritual disciplines as a path to holiness, but the disciplines come from love, and without love they are nothing. Given the truth that the church is the bride of Christ, I would say that real holiness comes from knowing my heavenly Father's love. Holiness comes from intimate connection with Jesus, rather than mere good theology. Holiness and intimacy with God are profoundly intertwined. We obey because we adore.

In Matthew 5, Jesus tells us that there is a joyful blessing for people who hunger and thirst for righteousness: they will be filled. The spiritually hungry can expect to be filled. The experience of holiness is the abundant life of fullness in Christ, not a legalistic list of dos and don'ts. The devil wants us to think holiness is boring, depressing, irrelevant, and restrictive. He wants us to see it as negative and limiting. He is the father of lies. Compromise is the devil's trick. I have never met a joyful lukewarm Christian, and I have never found peace trying to excuse my own sin. The lies of the enemy are subtle and we need to resist them. God is holy and He calls us to radical holiness. Jesus wants a bright, fiery church. We are all imperfect, broken people made holy through Jesus' precious blood shed on the cross. Holiness is not about rules and regulations, but is about seeking the Holy One.

Holiness is so beautiful, so glorious. When we encounter our holy God we are set free to be holy. Holiness is the brightness of God's radiance displayed in our lives. It is making God visible in our daily actions, reactions, and interactions. Holiness is the culture of heaven lived out practically on earth. Far from being restrictive, it brings wonderful liberty. The call to be holy in 1 Peter 1:16, "Be holy, because I am holy", is based on God's character and has power because His Spirit lives in us. The church has sometimes been embarrassed about holiness because of the desire to be more relevant, and as a result we have diminished our vision of God. Let's be relevant, but let's also be radically holy.

God's Jealous Love

The painful spiritual history of the Israelites is desperately sad. In Deuteronomy 4 we find a plea to flee from idolatry. God's heart was broken many times over an unfaithful people who had tasted of His goodness only then to return to idols, wickedness, and rebellion. Keeping God first stood at the very heart of the law. Deuteronomy 4:24 gives the summary that God's love is expressed in fiery jealousy. This jealousy is not like the sinful human emotion based on insecurity, fear, and anxiety. Rather, it is based on divine love, protection, and delight. How He loves us. This holy jealousy is zealous for us. God will not tolerate anything that comes between Him and us. He is a jealous God and we benefit immeasurably from His passion for us. Have we really understood God's love?

Have you ever thought of Jesus as jealous? This jealous love is a consuming fire; He is flawlessly holy and entirely loving. These perfections met at the cross. He is consuming fire and perfect love. We must be careful not to water down either of these truths. Many Christians struggle to see how God could love them, or even be interested in them. I believe that a revelation of God's holy jealousy for us would cure such doubt and low self-esteem. God loves us with such a love. O that we might taste and see the riches of His grace. He is jealous for us. He loves you.

Just in case you think this idea of God as a consuming fire was only present in the Old Testament, take a look at Hebrews

12:28–29 where we hear the call to worship in reverence and awe, for "our God is a consuming fire". The writer of Hebrews knows very well the history of God's people who encountered God on the fiery mountain and trembled. Our God is still a consuming fire. We worship God who is joy giver, Saviour, and also Judge of all. Holiness brings God's love, beauty, and judgments perfectly together. How great is our God.

What does a consuming fire look like? Well, put simply, it consumes! The fire of God burns against sin because sin separates us from God. Sin is a catastrophe. Our sin sent Jesus to the cross where He became sin. "God made him who had no sin to be sin for us, so that in him we might become the righteousness of God" (2 Corinthians 5:21). This consuming fire and holy jealousy cost God the life of His one and only Son. Jesus came to defeat our sin. The fire of God comes to burn up our sin.

The cross is the ultimate expression of our jealous God who consumes sin and loves sinners. Jesus tore every barrier down to bring us to Himself. The cross judged sin and took the punishment. None of us is holy through our own efforts, only through His blood. In relationship with consuming fire, we cannot hold on to our sin, even those sins we actually quite like. We can't willingly hold on to sin and be truly on fire for God. God's fire cleanses from sin and His jealous love will not share our hearts with other loves. He won't share first place with anything.

My Kingdom Go; Your Kingdom Come

Perhaps one of the greatest accounts of an encounter with divine God's holiness and jealous love is found in Isaiah 6. Isaiah had an awesome vision of God's glory filling the temple. In the vision, seraphim were calling out to each other:

> *"Holy, holy, holy is the Lord Almighty;*
> *the whole earth is full of his glory."*
>
> Isaiah 6:3

Then one of the seraphim came to Isaiah with a "live coal" from the altar. This coal was red hot. It was a burning coal and it represented the cleansing power of God's holiness. Such holy heat eradicates any impurities. The surprising thing about this vision for Isaiah was that it would have been painful! The coal actually touched him! Have you ever considered this? It touched his lips and as it did there was a declaration of forgiveness. Isaiah had become aware of his sin, as his sin had come into violent contact with the holiness of God. Contact with holiness hurts our compromise. This fiery coal was the way to cleansing.

God loves us too much to leave our sin intact. Sin must be expelled so love can be experienced. We can try to make the Christian life fit in with our enduring sin patterns, but sin must always be dealt with. The vision in the temple left Isaiah undone. This seems to be not very attractive to many people. It was an uncomfortable encounter. Who really wants to come to church to be undone by God and have their life turned upside down?

Somehow we have got the idea that holding on to areas of spiritual lukewarmness, coldness, sin, or selfish priorities is OK with Jesus. We like the idea of God as comforter, but not as consuming fire. Maybe God wants to consume sin that we might rather hold on to? Have you ever felt entitled to your anger, justified in your fear, and that you have a right to withhold forgiveness from *that* person? We cling to our self-centred offence and unforgiveness, we won't let go of our fear and pride, and we cuddle our selfishness and lust as though we expect it to be our comforter. If we hold on to sin, and even try to sanctify it or justify it, we will reap what we sow. Holiness is painful sometimes, but it is also wonderful. There are no shortcuts.

Maybe we have lost an understanding of holiness because we have softened sin and made some sins palatable. There are serious sins, which we are clever enough to avoid. But then there are secret sins of the heart that can be tolerated and even indulged. Those could include fear, control, pride, lust, greed, gluttony, not caring about the poor, and much more. How does that sound to Jesus? What would Isaiah's burning coal burn up in your and my life?

Let me add something very important here. There is no condemnation for those who are in Christ. Yes, we sin, but God forgives freely through Jesus Christ. I have often prayed the prayer of Robert Murry McCheyne: "God, make me as holy as it is possible for a saved sinner to be." I think we face a decision about freedom. Do we *really* want to be free? How much freedom are we hungry for? Do I actually want to be holy? Do I agree with God about my sin? Am I content to remain as I am?

We will never experience real breakthroughs in our freedom and holiness without a holy hatred for sin and a passion for Jesus. Again, this is based entirely on jealous love. The nineteenth-century preacher Thomas Chalmers preached a sermon on the "expulsive power of a new affection". Holiness is experienced through love. As 1 John 2:15 reminds us, "Do not love the world or anything in the world. If anyone loves the world, love for the Father is not in them." The apostle John made holiness an issue of love. I have a prayer that the Lord put in my heart more than ten years ago: "Lord, divorce me from secret sin." I want a divorce from sin. I hate sin because it keeps me from fully knowing, encountering, and reflecting Jesus.

Holiness affects everything: marriage, family, workplace, friendships, leisure, TV habits, what we read and eat, our dreaming and creativity, how we shop and consume. Holiness promotes justice, reconciliation, and peace. Roy Hession's book *The Calvary Road* has a section called "Holiness in the Home". Holiness is lived out with the people who know us best and love us most. I recently found these words of prayer in my journal from the 1990s:

Your eyes utterly piercing me,
Your heart jealously loving me,
Your blood fully cleansing me,
Your Spirit wholly possessing me.

The key to this challenge is that before we can pray, "Your kingdom come", we need to pray, "My kingdom go". Smith Wigglesworth used to sing a short song everywhere he went: "Emptied of self and filled with God."

But what does the consuming fire do? It devours, reveals, and consumes. Let's explore these three attributes more closely.

The Fire Devours

As I read the Bible's teaching about God's fire there is one theme that simply cannot be ignored. Most of the references to fire are in the context of God's judgment and wrath against sin. Let's take one example. Numbers 16:35 is not uncommon. It says, "And fire came out from the Lord and consumed the 250 men who were offering the incense." This verse comes in one of those chapters in the Bible which makes people feel very uncomfortable.

In Numbers 16, there was a rebellion against Moses and Aaron led by Korah and other Levites. God had vindicated Moses and Aaron by causing the earth to open up and swallow those who had opposed Moses and Aaron. Then fire came out from God's presence at the Tent of Meeting and devoured 250 Levites who were part of the rebellion and were making an offering with their golden censers. What are we to do with these difficult Scriptures? What is this about? These are verses that often bother us when we read the Bible, particularly the Old Testament. Is God being unfair in His holiness? We can't just ignore these verses. What can this mean for us today?

The truth is that the fire can devour and destroy. The God who sent His fiery judgment in Numbers 16 is the same God we worship today: Father, Son, and Holy Spirit. We must not take God lightly. Perhaps we have diminished the impact of sin and made God more compatible with our values. Therefore His fire causes us offence when it seems too harsh or unloving to us. We need to be careful about how we view God. These troubling Scriptures take nothing away from His love, mercy, and goodness. He is perfect in love and He is just when He judges. I can't emphasize enough the importance of having a right view of God, helping us to both understand and receive His fire.

Another Scripture, Psalm 50:3, declares, "Our God comes and will not be silent; a fire devours before him, and around him a tempest rages." What an awesome God! He is sovereign. He is powerful. He is able to defeat His enemies. This is seriously good news for us. I thank God that He will not be silent. Isn't it good that He is extreme in His opposition to sin and death? We should be glad that fire devours His enemies before Him. Who are these enemies of God? Sin, death, disease, demons, pain, and sorrow are defeated through Jesus.

I rejoice that the devil is a defeated foe through the sacrifice and resurrection of Jesus. The Lamb of God has overcome. Victory is a very powerful concept for the Christian journey. We are called to be victorious overcomers against the world, the flesh, and the devil.

We are living in a relentless spiritual battle today. The name Satan means "adversary". We have an adversary whose aim is to destroy everything holy and right. That is why it gives me joy and hope to read Scriptures such as Psalm 97:3: "Fire goes before him and consumes his foes on every side." This is our warrior God, the God we worship, strong in victory over the powers of darkness. Ephesians 6 is a potent reminder to us that we are part of that spiritual warfare. Putting on our spiritual armour and resisting the schemes of the devil are all part of Christian discipleship. We overcome through the weapons of salvation, righteousness, truth, the gospel, faith, prayer, and the Word of God. Love always wins and is the greatest weapon of all against evil. Jesus is always victorious. His name is higher than any other name. Take courage!

In the Old Testament when God consumed His foes, His people rejoiced. They were at ease with a God of judgment because He brought righteousness, justice, and hope. I believe we can learn something here. I totally trust God's judgment. More than that, I love, thank, and worship Him for His judgments, because they are part of His goodness. I see honouring God as Just Judge as part of what it means for us to fear the Lord. It is being able to worship God as victorious and majestic, yet this conquering Saviour, who devours sin, is our loving Father.

As a Father, I want to defend my family from all harm. I want to be victorious against anything that would seek to harm my three children. Would I stand by and watch them be harmed? No way! This is what so powerfully shows us our heavenly Father's goodness and grace. Not only that He gives good things to His people, but also that we are delivered from evil.

Think about it this way: Jesus is coming again, and His second coming will be very different to His first coming. At His first advent, Jesus came in obscurity, humility, and gentleness. When He comes again, it will be with power, fire, and glory. In Matthew 25:41, Jesus reminds us that the day of the judgment will be a day of fire, reward, and judgment. We will see the judgment of God displayed and He will destroy His foes on every side. We will worship Him because it is the Lord's doing. What would God be, if He were not just?

I feel it is important to pause here. I want to be very clear and honest with you. We don't take delight in any person being judged. There is absolutely no pleasure in knowing that some people will be lost and will experience the fire of God's judgment. The very opposite is true. It makes me desperately sad and implants a new urgency to share the gospel with people so they have the opportunity to come to Jesus. Love is at the heart of this chapter on holiness. Coming judgment is not a popular idea, but unpopularity does not change its impending reality.

Some people are gladly able to relate to the fire of Spirit, but not to the fire of judgment. They see the first as attractive and the other as cruel. I believe we need to repair this distortion. The fire of Pentecost comes from God and the fire that devours comes from God. Fire is not comfortable. But neither should we be fixated with judgment. Some people are unhealthily absorbed in judgment and sadly minimize God's kindness and grace. May God keep our hearts tender and soft so that they break with love for people who are still lost in sin without Christ. We need to let God be God – let Him be holy, just, and kind. We can trust His ways. He will do what is right for every person.

Here is one piece of great news about judgment. One day, the devil himself will be thrown into the lake of fire. Matthew 25:41 describes the scene where God will cast the devil into the "eternal fire prepared for the devil and his angels". This place of punishment is also described in Mark 9:43 as "hell, where the fire never goes out". A book on God's fire would not be honest if it did not mention hell. I agree with Francis Chan, who wrote in his book, *Erasing Hell*, that hell scares him.[2] I also agree with him that part of me really does not want to

2 Francis Chan, *Erasing Hell*, Colorado Springs: David Cook, 2011, p. 14.

believe in hell, but I do believe what the Bible says about hell as a place of eternal punishment and fire. Chan writes that God's judgments are not always easy to understand but, as Psalm 115:3 says, in the end God can do "whatever pleases him". As we wrestle with the devouring fire of God, we need to do so in prayer and humility, not with offence. Finding a way to worship and honour God through what we don't understand is all part of discipleship. To be honest, God doesn't owe you or me an explanation. God will not be taking lessons in justice from you or me any time soon.

What can we learn here? Not only that God is worthy of worship even when we don't understand everything, but also that there is no wisdom in sin. The devouring fire is a reminder that sin must be dealt with, and it reminds us of the glory of what Jesus did on the cross for us to save us from sin. Love defeats and devours sin. In the wisdom of God, His judgments are an expression of His love. His love tears down anything that keeps us away from God. Evan Roberts was right during the Welsh revival to emphasize confession of sin and the removal of every doubt from our lives. Father God, please devour anything not of You in my life. Let Your love devour sin.

The fire of God is literally for everyone. At some point in their lives, everyone will see and experience the fire of God. That is what the Bible teaches. It is our calling to so proclaim and demonstrate the gospel, to reveal the fire of His love and glory, rather than the people experiencing the devouring fire. Everyone is destined to experience the fire of Father God at some point, and everyone who calls on the name of Jesus will be saved.

The Bible sometimes bothers us. That is what makes it authentic. The Bible is honest with us about the reality of God and of our own condition. Before moving on, I want to call us to be very careful in our attitude to the fire of God's judgment. Let's keep our attitude and heart right on this. In Luke 9:54, some of the disciples got their attitude wrong when they said to Jesus, "Lord, do You want us to command fire to come down from heaven and consume them, just as Elijah did?" What was Jesus' reply? "But He turned and rebuked them, and said, 'You do not know what manner of spirit you are of. For the Son of Man did not come to destroy men's lives but to save them.'" (Luke 9:55–56, NKJV). Let's be careful to have the right attitude of love, mission, humility, and worship as we talk and pray about these things. Remember, God is good, all the time!

The Fire Reveals

The consuming fire of God's holiness also reveals and tests our hearts. This is another of God's mercies to us and another sign of His love and goodness. David knew the value of allowing the Spirit of God to search his heart. Psalm 139 describes his experience: "You have searched me, Lord, and you know me." David seemed to believe that this divine knowledge of him gave him security, protection, and intimacy, and increased his worship experience. David was not perplexed that God knew him so well. Rather than trying to hide from God, he invited the divine searchlight to shine into his innermost life. David gathered his thoughts in verse 17: "How precious to me are your thoughts, God! How vast is the sum of them!" This is a psalm of wonder and worship. God knows it all and He still loves me. What freedom there is in being both deeply known and deeply loved. I love this depth of honesty and connection with God.

Our culture places a high value on privacy. We are suspicious today of companies or individuals who want to know our private information. Their track record shows that they have not been great at keeping our confidence. When it comes to being known beyond the superficial level we reserve such privileges to very few. Perhaps only your spouse or close friends see you as you really are. We want to know that we really can trust those who know our innermost thoughts and struggles. Who could see me at my worst? Would they still love me? This is a huge question that most people are too afraid to seriously ask, let alone discover the answer to.

In 1 Corinthians 3:13, Paul makes a throwaway comment about the fire testing and revealing each person's work in a section of his letter dealing with divisions in the church. This is one of those topics in the Bible that we don't hear much about. When Paul says, "their work will be shown for what it is, because the Day will bring it to light. It will be revealed with fire, and the fire will test the quality of each person's work", he is teaching about building good foundations for eternity. He knows his foundations are solid because they were built on Jesus Christ. He goes on to say that anyone who builds on that foundation will have their work tested: "It will be revealed with fire". And the fire will "test the quality" of their work.

What is this revealing and testing about? It is quite a different way of seeing how God's fire works in our lives, and something we don't often think about. This fire seems to be able to reveal inner motivations and drivers for why we are who we are or have done what we have done. Many Christians don't even know that there will be a testing of the works we have done on earth, not according to human standards of excellence, but a testing that relates to the inner quality of heart and the real reason for that work. It will be very probing and revealing, and it seems that this fiery test will illuminate the truth about us. Jesus spoke of this time in Matthew 6, when He encouraged the people not to store up treasure on earth, but treasure in heaven. That treasure was built up through giving to the poor. We can become rich towards God and build up true treasure through genuine service and love.

What are we "building" with today? What are the drivers for our Christian obedience? Why do we serve people? What is going on in our hearts when we become involved in church or mission? Here is a reality check – everything we do for

God will be tested by fire which will reveal its quality. Are we seeking to build God's kingdom only to bolster our ego or to increase our standing in the community? Do we want people to look at us? Is there selfish gain in our ministry? There will come a day when we will stand before the judgment seat of Christ and all will be revealed by fire.

This truth of eternal reward has often been ignored, but Revelation 22:12 reminds us, "Look, I am coming soon! My reward is with me, and I will give to each person according to what they have done." Clearly there is an expectation of reward here. The revealing fire does not have to be negative or a fearful event. Paul's own assumption in 1 Corinthians 3 is that his work will be found to be of good quality. Right hearts will receive good rewards.

Salvation is a gift and is not earned by works, but the Bible seems clear that there is a reward for faithfulness to Christ and somehow suffering loss for unfaithfulness. While we are saved through the works of Jesus on the cross, we shall still appear at His judgment seat. This could not be clearer in 2 Corinthians 5:10: "For we must all appear before the judgment seat of Christ, so that each of us may receive what is due to us for the things done while in the body, whether good or bad."

Have I got your attention now? Romans 14:10–12 makes the same point. Speaking to Christians in Rome, Paul writes, "We will all stand before God's judgment seat ... So then, each of us will give an account of ourselves to God." This is not a judgment for sin, because that took place on the cross, where we were saved from sin past, present, and future (Colossians 2:13–15). Rather than being a judgment concerning the problem of sin, this is a testing by fire to discern eternal rewards. This is a judgment to celebrate victories won on earth; it is not a judgment that brings rejection for failure. However, the Bible does also give some insights concerning when the work is found wanting.

1 John 2:28 says, "And now, dear children, continue in him, so that when he appears we may be confident and unashamed before him at his coming." Then, completing the verses we started with in 1 Corinthians 3:14–15, we read, "If what has been built survives, the builder will receive a reward. If it is burned up, the builder will suffer loss but yet will be saved – even though only as one escaping through the flames."

According to 1 Corinthians 3, it is possible to be saved, to have sins forgiven, to go to heaven, and to inherit eternal life, but still to suffer loss. Wherever our works came from selfish motive or ambition, they will be burned up. Only what is done for Christ will last. The fire will test whether you were "building" for eternity or living for the moment on earth. As I read Scripture, I believe that even the things that failed in human terms yet were done for the glory of God will come forth as gold and will receive an eternal reward. Even works that did not necessarily succeed on earth will be rewarded because of the love in which they were done.

I would rather serve God "unsuccessfully" on earth with a heart of love and desire for God's glory than to seemingly succeed in works on earth but find it all burned up in heaven because my heart was full of selfish ambition or pride. Success in the kingdom of God is whatever passes through the fire. The flesh is stubble, hay, and wood that will be burned up and gone for eternity, even though you would still go to heaven by God's grace.

I want my life to bring forth fire-tested treasure for eternity. Such treasure looks like ordinary, small acts of love, service, and sacrifice. It looks like preferring others, seeking God in prayer, giving to the poor and needy, visiting the prisoners, healing the sick, mentoring the young person, sharing your faith with others, forgiving those who have hurt you, or going the second mile for someone who can't repay you. There are a million ordinary ways to live for eternity and receive the saint's reward. It's true that while man looks on the outward appearance, God looks at the heart (1 Samuel 16:7).

I have found the fire revealing my heart many times. God's idea of quality is not always about the end product, but about the character and love in the journey. Christian character needs fire, and fire will test its quality. This inspires me to live for the kingdom, to live a life of consuming holiness that endures the revealing fire, to the glory of God.

The Fire Consumes

It is good news that the fire of God devours, reveals, and consumes. Anything that reflects God's character is good news for us as believers in Christ. Our God is a consuming fire. Such fire utterly purges every impurity in its white-hot intensity and holiness. I love this fire. I thank God for such a fire that can burn away every trace of sin from my heart. I thank God that He does not tolerate anything that separates me from His holy presence. If God were passive or impotent to burn up and consume sin, where would our hope be?

This is our God – the consuming fire of holy love. He created us, pursued us, saved us, filled us, and will lead us home to glory, where He will reward us. What a wonderful Saviour. How the devil would desire to convince you that God's fire is pitiless, capricious, and unjust. His deceptions have led many Christians to question the very justice of God and to quibble about whether God is even fair. My dear friend, don't believe the lies of the enemy. Don't allow any distorted theology to lead you into doubting the goodness, justice, mercy, grace, and love of God.

I want to take a look at one more aspect of this consuming holy fire. It is the fire that consumes. In Leviticus 9:24 we read, "Fire came out from the presence of the Lord and consumed the burnt offering and the fat portions on the altar. And when all the people saw it, they shouted for joy and fell face down." This offering was the very first offering

Aaron had offered as priest, and the response of heaven was to send consuming fire.

What does this fire mean? The offering was acceptable to God. The sin of the people was covered. Joy came upon the people with the knowledge of sins forgiven. Do you see what good news this consuming fire brings? It is good news that the fire consumes, which is a picture of purifying people from sin. The people shouted with joy – they got it! They fell face down in thankful worship and surrender. What a response! Have you ever been in a church service where people were so excited that their sins are forgiven they shouted for joy and fell face down? I would love to see that more in church.

Repentance and forgiveness are the gateway to freedom. This scene in Leviticus was only a foretaste of the greatest day in history when Jesus gave Himself as the once-for-all offering that brought us into freedom through repentance and faith. Joy comes when we deal with sin. This is a picture of a people ablaze with freedom. They were face down in worship because they knew what it meant to have sins forgiven. This is why we need to allow the consuming fire to deal with any sin in our own lives. Compromise kills passion, but obedience ignites freedom. We are called to take hold of the liberty in which Christ has made us free.

There is freedom on the other side of cleansing. Many Christians today are hungry for freedom, but they forget that freedom comes through cleansing. Knowing the blessing of a clean heart is the place of liberty and freedom for you and me. What joy there is when there is mercy and grace; what worship when we are really free. The fire of the Lord has released the joy of the Lord. I believe we need to see much more joy and freedom in our churches today. Have you noticed that the same fire from heaven produces both judgment and joy?

Alone with God

Why not take some time to pray, reflect, kneel, worship, confess, reconnect, and decide by faith to go through with God. Let me pose three simple questions to you in the light of looking at God's consuming holy fire. You can use them to spend some time alone with God.

Am I holding on to persistent and wilful sin?

We all sin at times because, sadly, we choose to go our own way. Even in a split second, we can find ourselves caught in sinful thoughts, words, deeds, reactions, and actions. I believe one of the signs of Christian maturity is the length of time between our sin and our confession and repentance. Thank you, Lord, that when we fall into sin and repent and turn back, the blood of Jesus cleanses us. That is the promise of 1 John 1:9.

However, we need to be careful if we find ourselves in a place of wilful and sustained disobedience and hard-heartedness in persisting in the same sin, from which our conscience has diminished and we simply don't care that much. We all have battles with temptation and sin, yet if you determinedly choose wilful sin with no repentance, then, my dear friend, it is time to wake up and turn back to the Lord with all your heart.

What might the fire reveal about my life?

This is not theoretical. The day is coming when the fire will reveal our hearts before God. Better to obtain insight into that now and begin to live in the light of eternity and heavenly reward. How about taking some quiet time to reflect and pray? Ask the Lord to speak to you about His assessment of your life. It really is only His perspective that matters. You can read about Jesus doing this with the churches in Asia Minor in Revelation 2 and 3. I have made a useful and challenging study of what Jesus commended them for and also what He rebukes them for in those two chapters. What might Jesus say to you or your church?

Am I willing to be set on fire by a jealous God?

Psalm 69:9 says, "Zeal for your house consumes me". Am I willing to be consumed with that holy fire of God? Am I willing to be set on fire with His love? Am I willing to burn with His justice? Am I willing to die to self-centredness? He is jealous for you and me. He will not share us with idols we have made. The place of fire is the place of absolute surrender and power (Acts 1:8). Am I willing to surrender my life to Jesus? Am I willing to be holy no matter what it costs? Am I willing to repent from my sin and forgive everyone?

We are ordinary believers, with a mighty God. If you are like me, your heart cries, "Yes Lord," and yet we know we don't have the resources for such a life in our own strength. This is not about striving to be something impossible. The answer is the Holy Spirit. Consuming holiness comes through the Holy Spirit. Right now, though, spend time with God and do eternal business with Him in your heart.

Chapter 3

Receiving the Spirit of Fire

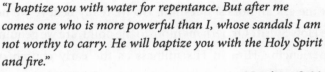

"I baptize you with water for repentance. But after me comes one who is more powerful than I, whose sandals I am not worthy to carry. He will baptize you with the Holy Spirit and fire."

Matthew 3:11

"Suppose we try Pentecost"[3]

Samuel Chadwick

Could God have made it any clearer? The gift of the Holy Spirit is for everyone who believes. Jesus brought salvation through His death and resurrection. Then He sent His Spirit upon the early church, so the promise spoken by John the Baptist in Matthew 3 was fulfilled in Acts 2. The fiery Holy Spirit came in power and He is still moving today. I believe the contemporary church needs a fresh baptism and filling with the Holy Spirit. Samuel Chadwick described this need:

Spirit-filled souls are ablaze for God. They love with a love that glows. They believe with a faith that kindles. They

3 Samuel Chadwick, *The Way to Pentecost*, Hodder & Stoughton, 1951, p. 19.

hate sin with a fierceness that burns. They rejoice with a
joy that radiates. Love is perfected in the fire of God.[4]

I believe that is the kind of church Jesus intended.

The Need to Sense Our Need

Let me ask an honest question. Do we really believe we need the Holy Spirit? Or perhaps more to the point, are we genuinely experiencing Him in His fullness as the early church did? Good theology without experience is like faith without works. Is there evidence in our lives of faith and love that can only be explained in terms of the work of the Holy Spirit?

Holy Spirit fire is needed to know fervency in prayer, passion in worship, power in evangelism, and love for the Scriptures. The Spirit of God desires to burn brightly in us. He wants to do signs and wonders that point to Jesus. He wants to empower holy living and clear witness and loving actions. He wants to reconcile families, restore marriages, feed the poor, and heal the sick. The Holy Spirit is the great need of the church. We have many great programmes, but our crying need is for God's power to enable us to live our lives more like Jesus.

There is so much more that is available through the ministry of the Holy Spirit than the church is currently experiencing. The gifts, fruit, and wisdom of the Spirit are not given as a top-up to make us feel good; they are given to transform the world

4 Chadwick, *The Way to Pentecost*, p. 43.

for the glory of God. The Holy Spirit is evidenced through a passionate church that is transforming lives, bringing glory to God, and serving others. He fills us to flow through us and so change nations.

Let me ask you again: do you believe in the Holy Spirit? Every Christian can experience the same fullness, empowering and joy as the first disciples did on the day of Pentecost. But the main outcome of Pentecost was seeing 3,000 people come to Jesus. It was not just an optional experience for some of the more enthusiastic disciples; it was a fiery outpouring of God's love and power on all of them. So do you believe in the Holy Spirit? Have you received the Holy Spirit in His fullness? The need has never been greater for a fresh outpouring of the Holy Spirit in our lives and churches. People energized by the Holy Spirit have urgency about evangelism, justice, and loving others. Indifference to God is impossible when we become flames of fire.

Do you agree that there is a lamentable lack of spiritual power in churches today across this nation? Even in evangelical and charismatic churches we have become so dulled by the familiarity of Acts 2 that we have lost the urgent cry to be filled with the Spirit, and not for ourselves, but for the advancement of the kingdom of God. Have we even noticed this absence of fire?

What was it that made the difference in people such as John Wesley, William Booth or Smith Wigglesworth? What was it that enabled them to lean into the impossible? They knew the secret of the fire of the Holy Spirit in their lives. Every one of these spiritual fathers had a clear story of the time when they were filled with the Spirit. As Chadwick describes, "Fire is self-evident."[5] You will know when you have been filled. Pentecost did not happen in a corner. It was not something quiet and hidden away from people. The disciples clearly were filled, and Jerusalem knew that those ordinary disciples now had a power that shook the city.

I believe it is time for us to wake up from our spiritual slumber. We need to shake off our fears about what people will think if we are filled with the Spirit. Why don't we overcome our reserve and passivity and cry out for fire from heaven over the church in our nation? We are afraid of the fire and so have settled for no fire at all. We need to sense our need. We need to wake up! We desperately need truly Spirit-filled Christians in this land. Men and women, boys and girls, in workplaces, hospitals, offices, schools, shops, streets, homes – everywhere, living in the power and love of the Holy Spirit. The church was intended to be on fire with love, captivated by holiness and passionate in serving and witnessing to Jesus.

Someone who has had a deep influence on my life is Revd Duncan Campbell from the Lewis Revival. He died more than forty years ago, but even as a teenager I would listen to his sermons every night. He saw a number of remarkable revivals in Scotland and Canada. In his biography, Andrew Woolsey

5 Chadwick, *The Way to Pentecost*, p. 18.

describes a time in Campbell's life when he realized that he was "busy in the Saviour's work, but a stranger to his intimate presence".[6] Campbell was filled with the Spirit and then saw revival. The greatest need is not necessarily more leadership seminars, slicker media outlets, increased staffing, or bigger budgets. We need the Holy Spirit. Have we forgotten the pure simplicity and power of the gospel? Let's be uncomplicated. I believe the answer to growing the church today is to see every person in our churches baptized by the Holy Spirit and fire.

Simplicity with Power

Is this a naive fantasy? I don't think so. I honestly believe we have watered down the gospel and the Holy Spirit to such an extent that we have forgotten our true identity and mandate as the church: to change nations. We have forgotten the power available through Pentecost because we have depended far too much on our own hard work and best efforts, rather than the Spirit of fire. Zechariah had it right when he declared, "'Not by might nor by power, but by my Spirit,' says the Lord Almighty" (Zechariah 4:6).

The gospel is not overly complicated; neither is the Holy Spirit. Jesus said the kingdom of heaven belonged to the little children. It belongs to the hungry, the poor in spirit, the broken, and those who know their great need of God. Please let's keep this simple and not too sophisticated with worldly

6 Andrew Woolsey, *Duncan Campbell: A Biography*, London: Hodder & Stoughton, 1974, p. 97.

wisdom. One of the marks of the kingdom is simplicity with power. The religious leaders in Jesus' day were marked by religious complication and powerlessness. The moment we make things too complex we have moved away from Jesus. It is costly, but not complicated. Jesus' ministry was marked by costly kingdom simplicity that transformed lives and communities.

You don't have to be clever, rich, or influential to be filled with the Spirit. All you need is found in the Lord Jesus Christ and what He has already done for us in His death, resurrection, and ascension. In Matthew 3, John proclaimed Jesus as the baptizer in the Holy Spirit. John the Baptist's ministry made a powerful impact, but it was only a foretaste of much greater to come. Jesus' ministry would release Holy Spirit fire on the earth.

There is much confusion about the term "baptism in the Spirit". That is because we have over-complicated it and therefore also missed it. Let me put it simply and clearly: it is the life of the Lord Jesus Christ poured out into our lives. The baptism of the Spirit is all about making us more like Jesus.

I love this description from Samuel Chadwick: "Do you want to know what the baptism of the Holy Spirit is? It is not a mere sentiment. It is not a happy sensation that passes away in a night. It is a baptism of love."[7] Describing the effect of the fire of God's Spirit on his own life, he writes:

7 Cited in S. Brengle, *Helps to Holiness*, Revival Classics, OTC Publishing, 2004, p. 13.

I praise Him! I adore Him! I love Him! My whole being is His for time and eternity. I am not my own. He can do with me whatever He pleases. I know that what He chooses must work out for my eternal good. He is too wise to make mistakes, and too good to do me evil. I trust Him, I trust Him, I trust Him.[8]

The Holy Spirit makes us like Jesus. That experience would birth a revolution in the church today. Can we see now the vital need for churches to be filled with the Spirit and become like Jesus? We would see such revival, growth, and freedom. We would be seeing people living for the kingdom. We need the fullness of the Spirit. As Oswald Chambers observed, "Pentecost did not teach the disciples anything, it made them the incarnation of what they preached."[9] This is the effect of receiving the Spirit. We are never the same again. The baptism of the Spirit gives the power to live out the message. Is this not the need in our church today? We know that there is so much that we are not living out. We need the Holy Spirit.

The greatest concern facing the church today is not numerical decline, struggling finances, extremist Islam, or aggressive secularization. Our greatest danger is lukewarmness. The early church had all our challenges and more, yet their answer came in fiery surrendered lives laid

8 Ibid, p14.
9 Oswald Chambers, *My Utmost for His Highest* (Barbour Publishing, Ohio), 1963, p.50.

down for Jesus Christ. The kind of reformation we need today is a revival of radical love and surrender. As I read the book of Acts, I see that kind of love, power, boldness, prayer, and urgency in the lives of the whole church. I see a church that was going through massive change and had real struggles, but was fearless because they were totally in love with Jesus. What are we waiting for?

No Substitute for the Holy Spirit

A few years ago, the Lord began showing me that even though I had what I thought was a balanced and healthy understanding of the Holy Spirit, in fact I was constantly replacing Him with my own resources. I want to be very open with you. I don't have all the answers or pretend to be perfect; I am still very much on a journey and in process in my Christian life. As I looked at my heart and reflected on my drivers and motivations, I could see that despite wanting to depend on God, I was in fact depending on myself and on proven techniques and principles to live my Christian life and lead others in church.

The Lord began to show me a number of substitutes by which I was living my Christian life, rather than by the Spirit. These substitutes seem harmless, even good. They can make us feel we are doing well and even being wise in leadership. However, over time, I grew tired of powerlessness. I began to think to myself, "I am not sure how much longer I can sustain this." This went on until I began to realize that I was trying to do in my own strength what could only be done in God's power.

For too long many leaders have worked in the strength of our natural resources. We get on with it. We manage; and there is a snare in being able to manage. We simply get tired and run out of steam. We have lost dependence on the Spirit's power. There is no substitute for the Holy Spirit. Jesus never lost that dependence. He was always doing the Father's will in the power of the Spirit.

Here are the substitutes I used. I have a hunch many other people rely on them too:

Striving and self-sufficiency

We so want to see God move that we end up trying to make it happen. I had a mindset that said, "If we could just … then we would see a difference!" and I would then throw my efforts into striving. This is not the same as pressing in to God. Striving is driven by performance-based acceptance. It leads to frustration, anxiety, anger, and burnout.

I find it interesting that the human resources of the church have never been so great. Our opportunities are endless and the need is overwhelming, yet why is there so little fruit? Much of the reason, I suspect, is that striving produces no kingdom fruit. It is a hard taskmaster based on working *for* God, not *with* God. Striving shows the attitude of a slave, not of a son or daughter of God.

Religious form

The religious substitute says, "It worked this way before, so we will do it again." There is no dependence here because we don't need to ask or find out how to do something. We just do what we have done before. We trust in precedents, systems, structures, and formulae.

Have you noticed how Jesus ministered in so many different ways and how He depended on His Father's voice to know what to do? In John 5:19, Jesus gives us an insight into His approach to ministry. He says, "Very truly I tell you, the Son can do nothing by himself; he can do only what he sees his Father doing, because whatever the Father does the Son also does." Jesus does nothing by Himself! Read the gospels and you will see how Jesus healed people in many different ways, in response to what His Father was doing. This is the opposite of religion, which has form but is without power (Matthew 22:29 and 2 Timothy 3:5).

The Pharisees were experts in the form of religion, but lacked power. Sadly, I recognize the same tendency in me. I find a model that works and stick with it, even if it is less fruitful next time. What God said to do in one event may not be what we need to do at the following event. We need to depend on Him more rather than trusting in ourselves. Being on fire for God means we will be less formulaic. Where there is no power, there is no gospel.

Natural wisdom

This one is subtle because it seems so sensible. It is depending on common sense and general principles as the guide for life and ministry. This is not to discount the wisdom that comes from common sense and learning from past experience. However, as outlined in 2 Corinthians 2:6–16, wisdom comes from being taught by the Spirit.

The issue is that often we simply decide what we think is best and ask the Lord to bless it. Is that God's way to live? What are we depending on – our past experiences or the Holy Spirit? We need to keep asking the Lord for His wisdom on a daily basis. His wisdom will not always align with common sense. God doesn't always do what we might reasonably expect from a common-sense perspective.

Hard work

Here's how this goes. If we put the hours in, something will happen, and if nothing happens, we just work a little harder. This one is also very subtle, because rather than being based on grace, it makes us try to earn blessings. This is not the gospel.

Hard work is right and it is good to be diligent, but work alone does not bring fruitfulness. We can't spiritually transform communities simply by sheer hard work. God works best when we are at rest. In John 15, Jesus' command is to abide, not to work hard. It is to draw close, not to try harder. That is key to real fruitfulness. Jesus commended the

Ephesian church in Revelation 2 for their hard work, but they had forsaken Him as their first love. God's wisdom values love over labour.

May we relinquish these pale substitutes and remember the truth that we can live in the power of the Spirit. Many people testify that after receiving the fullness of the Spirit they went home and did the same things as before, but with new power. Dependence on the Spirit is the path to power.

How Can I Be Filled?

You can be filled with the Spirit. Joel 2 and Acts 2 remind us that the promise is for you. The fire of God was always external in the Old Testament – on the temple, in the camp, or in judgment. Now in the New Testament the fire came upon them and burned within them. This had never been seen before. This fire from heaven recorded in Acts 2:3 was totally new. The fire of the Spirit possessed them.

The fire of God is meant to burn in you. You were made to be full of the Spirit. The centre of the Christian faith is "Christ in you, the hope of glory" (Colossians 1:27). He is in you by the Holy Spirit. As Christians, our bodies are temples of the Holy Spirit (1 Corinthians 6:19). God came to dwell within you at salvation, and He longs to go on filling you. This is the clear teaching of Ephesians 5:18, that we are to go on being filled with the Spirit. This filling is a clear, continual command, and it is available by faith today.

Perhaps you have never heard you can be filled? Maybe you have known that filling in the past but have now grown distant and cooled down spiritually? God is today calling you to come to Him to be filled afresh with His fullness.

So many times, when I have given a call for people to come forward after hearing a message on the Holy Spirit, I have seen people respond. At that moment there is an enormous desire in their hearts to be filled, yet I often wonder what will happen to that desire within the next few hours and days. What happens to the commitment they offer? Is there a hunger to follow through on Monday morning? Some people are continually crying out for more, but do not make progress. I sometimes feel that this lack of forward movement is because of the constant cry for more of God without surrendering to Him. We have to follow through on our spiritual passion and translate it into obedience. For me, the prayer, "More, Lord" goes both ways. Yes, we are asking for more of His presence, grace, and intimacy, but we are also giving more of ourselves as best we know how. More surrender and more obedience: these are key to walking in the fullness of God.

This reminds me of the need today for fiery spiritual fathers and mothers to show us the way. I always find it really helpful when I can see someone ahead of me in the Christian life, so I can imitate their way of life and faith to help draw me closer. That is the role of these spiritual fathers and mothers. Maybe you are called to be one? To follow

Jesus and be on fire yourself and so inspire, mentor, and help others follow Him.

Let me share a few characteristics of the person God is looking to fill with His Spirit. If you cultivate these biblical characteristics in your life, you will be filled.

Brokenness and humility

At its heart, this is about deep honesty with God. Where am I with God? Am I in right relationship with Him? Is there anything coming between us? Being broken is about laying down our pride and self-sufficiency. It is coming to the humble place of deep desire and thirst for God's fullness in my life. When we are broken, we know we need God.

Brokenness starts at the cross. Jesus was broken. He laid down His life and did not resist His call to die. Brokenness is not about feeling hopeless or worthless; it is the opposite. Brokenness is seeing the worthiness of Jesus and finding an honest place where all we want is to glorify Him and live for Him at the expense of all our earthly ambitions and pleasures. It is a heart posture of repentance, coming to the end of ourselves and turning to Christ with our whole lives.

Brokenness is essential because being filled with the fullness of God will take us to servanthood, not the seeking to be centre of attention. Brokenness is about death of sin and self and about the release of a holy beauty in our hearts that is so attractive to the Holy Spirit. He loves to fill broken people.

Psalm 51:17 declares, "My sacrifice, O God, is a broken spirit; a broken and contrite heart you, God, will not despise." This is heart preparation for being filled. It is not easy, but it is glorious.

Joyful obedience

I fear some people see the filling of the Spirit as an ecstatic experience for its own sake. In other words, while there must be an experience of the Spirit that is powerful, they see the experience as an end in itself. That is why today there are many who just look for one spiritual high after another. While there is a necessity to experience the Spirit, the experience itself is only a means to the end of knowing Christ more, and when we know more of Him, we will keep His commandments. This is the clear teaching that runs through Jesus' ministry, especially John 15. My will must bend to His will. Obedience is clearly linked to intimacy and experience. Loving God is an emotion, but it is also a choice to obey and become His disciple.

Years ago I spotted an amazing verse about the Holy Spirit that has always stayed with me. Acts 5:32 describes the Holy Spirit as the one "whom God has given to those who obey him". The Holy Spirit is given in response to our obedience. It is one of those conditional promises of Scripture. Our obedience moves God. To everyone who says they are hungry for more of God, I want to ask, are you willing to obey Him in everything? God will give the Spirit to us as we give ourselves to Him. The first time I knew the fire of the Spirit was at the moment of full surrender.

Breathe on me, breath of God
Till I am wholly Thine;
Until this earthly part of me
Glows with Thy fire divine.[10]

Waiting upon God until He comes

Sometimes people crowd the front of the church in response to an appeal and spend just a few moments asking God to fill them. Then they go for coffee and chat with others and then on to Sunday lunch, and wonder why they are not yet filled.

I have already spoken of the significance of the call to wait and pray in Acts 1. You may be wondering why you are not filled, but God may be asking you to wait upon Him in prayer. How much do we want the Holy Spirit? Waiting is about increasing hunger and expectancy. This is one of those simple truths that cannot be bypassed. We must wait in prayer. This means getting on our knees and spending time with God.

Seeking the fullness of the Spirit may be very emotional, but it is not about seeking an emotion. It is about seeking God Himself, and we must be prepared to spend time in His presence, getting to know Him. The first disciples waited for ten days in prayer before Pentecost. Are we willing to wait in prayer?

10 Edwin Hatch, "Breathe on Me, Breath of God", 1878.

Asking in expectant faith

Jesus promised the Holy Spirit. He longs to pour out the Spirit on all flesh. It is important to ask so that you might receive (Matthew 7:7–8). This is a promise to everyone. Many have downgraded God's purposes for our lives. Let's be all God created us to be and ask for His fullness. As John Sweney wrote so simply:

Fill me now, fill me now,
Jesus come and fill me now;
Fill me with your Holy Spirit,
Come, O come and fill me now.[11]

Make this your prayer. I sing it often, as I know how I need the constant filling of the Spirit. I need the fresh fire of holiness, revival, purity, and refining. Ask Him right now, and go on asking.

The fiery baptism of the Spirit is not a supercharged optional extra. Baptism is interesting language because it usually signifies water. But it is in fact a wonderful image. The Spirit of God is described as both fire and water in Scripture. The meaning of baptism of fire, as I see it, is about being saturated in the fire of God – soaked in fire. This baptism is for you and for me. It is irresistible, uncontrollable, unstoppable, and indispensable.

11 John Sweney, "Hover O'er Me Holy Spirit", 1879.

O for a passionate passion for souls,
O for a pity that yearns,
O for a love that loves unto death,
O for a fire that burns,
O for the pure prayer power that prevails,
That pours itself out for the lost;
Victorious prayer in the Conqueror's name,
O for a Pentecost.

Amy Carmichael

Chapter 4

Hungry for Revival Fire

*When Solomon finished praying, fire came down from heaven
and consumed the burnt offering and the sacrifices, and the
glory of the Lord filled the temple ... When all the Israelites saw
the fire coming down and the glory of the Lord above the temple,
they knelt on the pavement with their faces to the ground, and
they worshipped and gave thanks to the Lord, saying,*

*"He is good;
his love endures forever."*

2 Chronicles 7:1, 3

My heart was first awakened to revival as a teenager. I came to Christ through a mission called the Faith Mission. This was the same mission organization that Duncan Campbell worked with during the Lewis Revival of 1949. Through my connections with that mission, I began to read stories of remarkable moves of God in communities around the UK and overseas. I met people who had been converted during such times of revival, and a seed was sown in my heart. I looked at my experience of church as I had grown up and I knew we were not seeing the kind of blessings I had heard about. I wanted to see revival. It was great to see trickle growth in church, but I knew there was more. What I read stirred up a hunger in me. What God had done then, He could do again.

In 2008 I went to the New Wine leaders' conference where God spoke powerfully to me. By this time I had been ordained for a few years and the vision I had felt as a teenager had not gone, but it was on the back burner. I can remember sitting in the venue when God touched me with the words, "I was born for revival." This resonated deeply with my spirit. I wept as I realized that I still carried that fiery longing for revival, but I had become disconnected from that calling over the past few years as I had been getting on with church ministry. I had lost a heart passion to see God move in revival blessing.

That morning, God reconnected my heart to the great need in our nation and my longing to be part of a generation that sees the greatest move of God the UK has ever seen. This generation is hungry for a move of God that will change the face of the church and the nation, that the church may shine much brighter than ever before.

The greatest need in our generation is revival. When I think of revival and pray for it, I see a manifestation of God in our communities and nation. This is now a vision deeply imprinted in my heart. I see that revival every day as I walk the streets of my own community of Loughton in West Essex. Nothing short of a demonstration of God will meet the needs today.

It's Time for Revival

I have led St Mary's Church in Loughton for several years, and our vision as a church family is for revival. We want to see every person and every place saturated with God. We love

Loughton and long to see transformation of our town, region, nation, and beyond. Our desire is for the whole community to meet God. We want to be a town where the community becomes God-conscious.

Without knowing Jesus, our nation is lost and without hope. Millions upon millions have no thought of God. Have we really seen the extent of the need today? If we believe that the Bible teaches that people are lost without Jesus and will face the judgment of hell, then we will find a new loving urgency to see as many people as possible come to salvation and to know God. Not only is there a grave spiritual urgency, but also when we reflect on social needs today such as poverty, isolation, abuse, addiction, violence, and a thousand other varieties of need, we long to see a demonstration of God's power affecting the community to meet that need.

Even with our best efforts in evangelism, we still only really see small numbers of people coming to faith and healing in Christ. Revival is much more than evangelism. We need a mighty move of God in our communities that will draw many thousands into the kingdom of God. In 1859, which has been described as "the Year of Grace", more than 500,000 people came to Christ in England. Evan Roberts had a similar vision for revival in Wales. He pleaded with God for 100,000 people to be saved in that year. What is our vision? Do we long to see a mighty move of God in our time? I believe it is time for revival. We need the fire from heaven.

What is revival? First, there is personal revival, which is the life of Jesus filling us and renewing us. Roy Hession writes, "Revival is the Lord Jesus poured into human hearts."[12] That is its essence. God comes and moves in love, power, goodness, and holiness. That is why it is associated with fire. We are still living in the effect of the Pentecost revival. Revival is the life of Jesus poured into us.

Secondly, revival also means God powerfully touching a community and releasing His manifest presence in such a way that many people turn to Christ. This revival is new life flowing where spiritual life has ebbed. This often occurs when people have found personal revival and the presence of God outpouring into the wider community. The supernatural realm and power of God become so real that God cannot be ignored and the community seems utterly saturated with God and alive to the gospel.

Fire Came Down from Heaven

There are many accounts of the revival fire of God in Scripture. Biblical revivals under Old Testament kings included times of refreshing through Asa, Josiah, Jehoshaphat, and Hezekiah. These were times when, to some extent, the nation came back to God and God swept in with blessing.

Let's look at one such remarkable move when the fire of God fell in revival blessing in 2 Chronicles 7. As I read these

12 Roy Hession, *The Calvary Road*, London: CLC, 1950, p. 11.

passages I feel stunned by the scene. To think that these events took place even under the old covenant is incredible. We have access to the more glorious fire of God through the new covenant and Pentecost. 2 Chronicles 7 describes an incredible worship service, as King Solomon dedicates the temple for worship and sacrifices. This temple would have been a stunning building, but the furnishings impressed no one that day. It was the awesome fire and presence of God that captivated people.

Solomon finished his dedication prayer in verse 1 and "fire came down from heaven". What a sight! What an effect that prayer had! One man's prayer changed his nation. Fire fell from heaven and consumed the burnt offering and sacrifice, and the glory of the Lord filled the temple. The glory and presence of God was so weighty and heavy that the priests could not get into the temple. This is powerful. What an atmosphere of glory, power, and love. I would love to see this in our churches today: the presence and glory of God made manifest in the community.

This brief and magnificent story gives us a number of insights into genuine revival. It shows us some marks of God moving in power that we can learn from today. Let me describe them as four characteristics of what God restores to the church in revival:

An enlarged appetite for prayer

The fire of God came in answer to prayer. Prayer is as vast as the purposes of God. It is the road to blessing and key to revival. This is why the Chinese church continues to be strong in revival. The people pray bold prayers! They know how to shift the spiritual atmosphere through prayer. This is the secret of revival. We need to learn this ministry of prevailing prayer.

Duncan Campbell writes of this experience:

I could take you to a little cottage in the Hebrides and introduce you to a young woman. She is not educated; one could not say she was polished in the sense that we use the word, but I have known that young woman to pray heaven into a community, to pray power into a meeting. I have known that young woman to be so caught in the power of the Holy Spirit that men and women around her tremble – not influence, but power.[13]

That young woman has much to teach us about prayer.

A deeper awareness of God

We read that the glory of the Lord filled the temple. Revival always brings the glory to God. No church, personality, preacher, or person should come between God and His glory. In revival, the presence of God is everywhere. I believe revival restores that valuing of the presence and glory of God. It cures our obsession with self and puts God at the centre. We so need

13 Duncan Campbell, *The Price and Power of Revival*, London: Scripture Illustrations Ltd, 1956, p. 45.

that fresh sense of the awareness of His manifest presence. Cultivating a love for His presence brings revival to our souls. Many churches have good programmes, but I long for more churches that value His presence.

A robust attitude to sin

The fire came and consumed the sacrifice and offering. So the first thing the fire did was to deal with sin. Sin separates us from God, and when the fire of God comes into our churches and communities, God will deal with it robustly. Romans 3:23 tells us that sin makes us "fall short of the glory of God", while revival is an outpouring of His glory. Revival always produces holiness and a holy hatred for sin. This springs from His heart of love because God longs to release people from sin into freedom. I have always found Psalm 51 a great psalm to pray through when I confess and deal with sin in the light of God's purity. Let's not make excuses for our sin any more. Revival restores us to the glory through deep conviction of sin and the resulting blessing of forgiveness and a clean conscience.

A powerful revelation of God's goodness

Perhaps the most remarkable scene in this passage is how the priests and people knelt on the pavement with their faces to the ground and worshipped. Something wonderful had happened. God had come. There was no inhibition. The only fitting response was to bow down prostrated in the breathtaking presence of such an awesome God. Bowing in the dust they cried out together, "He is good; his love endures forever." What a revelation in that moment – God is good! This is the God who wants to invade our communities. He is so good. His love endures forever. In revival, the goodness of God comes to the fore. His love pervades the atmosphere in the community. People need to see God as He really is. He is good. His love endures. This is revival.

I with all my heart long for the day when the presence of God so pervades our communities that we can do nothing but get on our faces in the streets, churches, schools, shops, GP surgeries, and homes, and find people everywhere crying to God for mercy. Is this not the answer to the need in our nation? God is able to turn people's hearts back to Himself. He is able, in answer to a praying people, to manifest His glory in our communities. He has done it many times before and He can do it again. I would strongly encourage you to read the histories of revival in Britain and around the world. You will never be the same again.

An Awakening Atmosphere

Recently, I had the honour of meeting up with some people who were converted to Christ during the Lewis Revival. As we shared, there was such a holy solemnity and sense of God's presence. I will never forget meeting them and hearing their experiences. There was a precious and hushed sense of God's glory along with weeping as they shared their testimonies and their great desire to see revival again.

One man, now a retired minister, described the pervading atmosphere of eternity on the island as a "breath from heaven". He described the movement as though Jesus had come to stay in the villages. The presence of the Lord was everywhere. There was a light around the Christians and they did not want to part company. Many "after meetings" were held in homes until two or three o'clock in the morning. "What meetings!" they said. There was a lot of weeping and people had a real concern for their souls. Nothing would keep people from meeting together. They met each night to praise and pray. The singing was glorious. Some people saw doves descending on those who were about to give their lives to Christ. There was family worship in homes and prayer meetings were crowded. The whole atmosphere was full of God. People came from everywhere. Many were saved before they even came near a meeting.

I remember the first time I read about Peggy and Christine Smith of the Isle of Lewis. They were both in their eighties and suffering from severe medical conditions, yet they were mightily used by God in prayer. God had given them a vision of churches crowded with young people, and they grasped the promise of God from Isaiah 44:3, to "pour water on the thirsty land, and streams on the dry ground". They continued in prayer three nights a week until two in the morning.

Here is one account of the prayer breakthrough: "We struggled through the hours of the night refusing to take a denial. Our God is a covenant-keeping God. Did He fail us? Never. Before the morning light we saw the enemy retreating and our wonderful Lamb take the field."[14] That evening the revival breakthrough came. We need this in our churches and nation today.

Duncan Campbell describes a young elder in the church who realized that he was not in right relationship with God, even though he was praying for revival, and he saw his need for "clean hands and a pure heart" (Psalm 24:3–4). Campbell describes that prayer releasing a power that shook the parish from centre to circumference: "An awareness of God filled the barn and a stream of supernatural power was let loose in their lives. They had moved into a new sphere of God-realization, believing implicitly in the promise for revival."[15] They went out to find the whole community ablaze with God. It is consecration that brings visitation.

In his book of revival sermons, Duncan Campbell describes revival as, "The going of God among His people, and an awareness of God laying hold of the community."[16] He said that, to the praying men and women of Barvas in the Isle of Lewis, four things were clear, and these things became guiding principles of the movement:

- They themselves must be rightly related to God.
- The conviction that God is a covenant-keeping God and He keeps the promises in His Word in answer to prayer.

14 Wesley Duewel, *Revival Fire*, Grand Rapids: Zondervan, 1995, p. 309.
15 Woolsey, *Duncan Campbell*, p. 115.
16 Duncan Campbell, *God's Answer: Revival Sermons*, Edinburgh: The Faith Mission, 1960, p. 72.

- They must be prepared for God to work in His own way, not according to their programme. They believed in the sovereignty of God, but that did not relieve them of their responsibility.
- There must be a manifestation of God, demonstrating the reality of the Divine in operation.

Campbell describes that revival as the supernatural working of God in a community. He describes seeing some people

> *weeping under conviction of sin and others with joy and love filling their hearts, falling upon their knees, conscious only of the presence of God. Within a matter of days the whole parish was in the grip of a spiritual awakening. Churches became crowded with services continuing until 3am. Work was largely put aside as young and old were made to face eternal realities.*[17]

He goes on to say:

> *The most remarkable feature of this gracious visitation was not what happened in church, but the spiritual impact made on the island. People who until then had no thought of seeking after God were suddenly arrested and became deeply concerned about their soul's salvation.*[18]

17 Campbell, *God's Answer*, p. 76.
18 Campbell, *God's Answer*, p. 86.

Revival is God's answer to the desperate needs in our nation today. How I long to witness such scenes in my own parish and community. What if such fire spread today? Imagine your church and community in the grip of God. What would an awakening atmosphere look like in your community? God will show you on your knees.

Then the Fire of the Lord Fell

Then you call on the name of your god, and I will call on the name of the Lord. The god who answers by fire – he is God!

1 Kings 18:24

Then the fire of the Lord fell and burned up the sacrifice, the wood, the stones and the soil, and also licked up the water in the trench.

1 Kings 18:38

Our God is the God who answers by fire. Here in the book of 1 Kings, Elijah faces an entirely different scene from that which had faced King Solomon, but the same fire of revival comes in answer to earnest prayer and outrageous courage.

This was far from being a worship service in the temple: Elijah was facing a desperate crisis in the nation. It was a time of idolatry, intimidation, conflict, and persecution in Israel. Some prophets were hiding from Ahab and Jezebel. Into this conflict came the prophet Elijah. He stood and challenged the false prophets of Baal. This was also a time of famine because of Elijah's word that there should be no rain. These were desperate days, and Elijah took his stand in opposing the powers of darkness, which were out to defy God.

I can't help but see similarities with our situation in the nation and the church today. I believe we are also in a desperate situation. I often hear preachers heralding and celebrating the "current revival". But I have to be honest and say that we are not in true revival at the time I write. Yes, there are great encouragements and many wonderful testimonies of the gracious moving of God among individuals. But our communities and nation as a whole remain unmoved. There are forces of postmodernism, secularism, consumerism, and materialism that are drowning the nation, and in many cases the church as well. We have moved far from biblical values in Britain and our ethical values are becoming unrecognizable, for example with the recent legal redefinition of marriage. It is now not inconceivable that Christians may face more open persecution in this country, simply for proclaiming biblical truths which were until recently widely held.

But our God is the God who answers by fire. The God of Elijah is alive and He is still answering prayer. God knows how to turn people's hearts back to righteousness. Let there be a demonstration of fire: penetrating, illuminating, burning; making God real. Elijah's challenge was bold and made even more impossible by pouring water over the altar. In verse

37, he prays that the answer will show that God is "turning their hearts back again". Then, in answer to Elijah's brief but earnest prayer, the supernatural fire of God fell. This answer from heaven was a visible demonstration of the power, truth, and love of God. It was open for all to see and it changed the nation. God had swept in.

Think about your community. See the shops, homes, and businesses. What would it look like for the fire of the Lord to fall in your community? What challenges are you facing? What would a manifestation of the glory and power of God look like? See your streets with people kneeling as people are crying out to God for mercy. Think of your supermarket with God sweeping in. Is God calling you to be an Elijah? Is God calling you to be a Solomon? Are you saying today, "I believe I was born for revival"? Do you have a burning heart for your community to see God? Duncan Campbell once said, "It is wonderful to be in a place or community when you are made conscious of the fact that God has swept in. That the fire of the Lord has fallen and you can have no doubt whatsoever about it."[19] I believe this is what is needed in our day. Oh that we might see it. We need the fire from heaven.

19 Duncan Campbell, "The Fire of God", Available at www.sermonaudio.com/sermoninfo.asp?SID=5290774229 (accessed 20 July 2015).

Nothing is Impossible with God

This chapter feels like an enormous challenge to me. Part of me struggles with unbelief as I question how it could ever be that God would move so powerfully in our nation today. Sometimes I think to myself that it was fine for people in days gone by, the Christians of yesteryear. Revival just seems so big that it is difficult to grasp. Could such a thing really happen here? Might I see it? Surely not: it is too wonderful, too fantastic, too big. I have to be honest that, despite my longings, I often struggle with this. Is this dream and vision for revival all in vain?

But although the problems in our nation are so great and the darkness intense, our God is still the God who answers by fire. The God who visited Solomon's temple and invaded their worship service is alive. The God who descended on Elijah's altar and whose fire even licked up the water-soaked sacrifice is alive, and He is still in the business of sending fire today.

Our church, St Mary's Loughton, holds on to the Scripture in Luke 1:37, that "nothing is impossible with God" (NIV 1984). These words were spoken to Mary by the angel Gabriel as he told her how God would become man and how the plan of salvation would unfold through the baby to be conceived in her womb. What an impossibility Mary had to comprehend. Sometimes we can't really understand or fully take in what God can do. He is not asking us to understand, but simply to obey by faith. And to come into agreement with Him. Maybe we don't need to worry about understanding revival and the way God sends His fire; we just need to exercise faith to believe and obey.

How, then, can we begin to think about seeing this happen? What does this faith and obedience look like as we long for the fire from heaven to visit us in the twenty-first century? I believe revival is birthed in prayer, and it is so encouraging to see now a worldwide movement of prayer that is growing. Our brothers and sisters in the developing world have led the way in this prayer movement, which I am sure will result in worldwide revival.

Prayer is central, but let me share something equally as challenging, which I believe is also a key for seeing revival come.

Revival Begins at Home

Something the Lord showed me a couple of years ago was that revival begins at home. I was at a leaders' conference in central London and went forward for prayer ministry. There were so many responding that I knew it would be a long time before anyone came to pray for me, so I began to pray by myself, and in the next few moments the Lord took me into what I believe was a vision. It is the only vision I have ever seen, but I think it was a vision. It was certainly more real than a faint picture. In this vision, I was standing in front of our vicarage, our family home next to the church. I can remember trying to turn around to see the church, but I could not. The Lord was showing me my home.

Then I saw that my home was submerged underwater. It was as though it was under a river, which I felt was the river of God and a symbol of the Holy Spirit. Then I began to realize that God wanted to move powerfully in my family. I am married to Caroline and we have three beautiful children who all know the Lord. I believe God spoke to me about His desire for revival in my home before bringing revival to the church. More than that, there was a sense that revival in my home would bring revival in the church. The birthplace for revival was in the home. I had come to the leadership conference looking for a few more principles to help me lead the church family, but what God gave to me was a vision to lead my own family into revival. I had not expected that at all.

I love Roy Hession's classic book on holiness and revival, *The Calvary Road*. There is a chapter in that book entitled "Revival in the Home" which was a powerful challenge to me. He wrote, "It was into the home that sin first came. It is in the home that we sin more perhaps than anywhere else, and it is in the home that revival first needs to come … a revived church without revived homes would be sheer hypocrisy."[20] The home is the place where there can be a great deal of hardness of heart. It can be a place for irritations, tempers, and selfishness. In our homes do we find a lack of love, an inability to be real

20 Hession, *The Calvary Road*, p. 62.

with one another, and a tendency to be easily angered? If so, then surely we need revival in our own homes as the starting place for revival in our communities and nation. That is a vision and a challenge to us all – including me! Nothing is impossible with God.

When it comes to preparing for revival, I want to return to 2 Chronicles 7. In that chapter is one of the best Scripture verses I know to help us. It is verse 14: "If my people, who are called by my name, will humble themselves and pray and seek my face and turn from their wicked ways, then I will hear from heaven, and I will forgive their sin and will heal their land." If we begin to live that out in our experience, God will be true to His promise and we will see His fire in our day and in our time.

Chapter 5

Passing through Refiner's Fire

He said, "Look! I see four men walking around in the fire,
unbound and unharmed, and the fourth looks like a son of
the gods."

Daniel 3:25

Learning from the Persecuted Church

Recently something wonderful happened in our church that
was unexpected. Within a few months we had three separate
opportunities to welcome and host brothers and sisters in
Christ from Syria, China, and Iran – all countries where the
church is being persecuted. This was not something we had
sought. We did not go out to find persecuted Christians; they
just seemed to keep coming to us. It didn't take too long before
we realized God was speaking to us.

Our friends from Syria were extraordinary. A pastor and his
wife came with humble and Christlike hearts. Their testimony
about the power of full surrender to Christ and their practice
of prayer and fasting really had an impact on us. Brother Yun
came to us from the Chinese underground church, and his
was a message of uncompromising commitment to witness
to the risen Christ and to use every opportunity given to us

to make Jesus known. Then two amazing women who had lived in Iran witnessed powerfully about how love for Jesus superseded everything else in their lives, so they could never deny Him. Their passionate love for Jesus poured forth, and as a church we knew God was speaking to us.

Generally speaking, we live such comfortable lives in the West. No doubt there are many deep and pressing social problems, but compared to the developing world, we have so much. I believe that through these visits the Lord was calling us to increased dependence on Him and decreased reliance on ourselves.

We were being shown a model of what living for the kingdom looked like. My wife Caroline has a real passion for Jesus-centred simplicity. We have so much we don't even need and it brings a fog into our lives that blocks out kingdom living. We are so wedded to shopping, ownership, and self-improvement that we miss the real deal of justice, love, and mercy, and of meeting the much greater needs in our local and global world. The worship of our stuff is strangling the life out of the real practice of our faith in Jesus.

What can we learn from our brothers and sisters who do not defend their rights, but rather use their opportunities in prison for their faith to share the gospel with other prisoners? What can we learn from the persecuted church that grows exponentially every year but has no websites, publicity, or buildings? What can we learn from a church that regularly fasts and prays? What can we learn from a church where leaders get up at 5 a.m. every day to pray? Is it any wonder revival is spreading where there is persecution? We have much to learn from our brothers and sisters who have been living for the kingdom in the refiner's fire.

I believe the refiner's fire is never far from the person who wants to serve the purpose of God in their generation. I have often been amazed that when God moves in a person's life, there is often an accompanying level of persecution, opposition, and testing. Finding favour with God and persecution from the world seem to go together. Consider Jesus' mother Mary and the difficulties she encountered immediately after being told she was highly favoured by God and would bear the Son of God. Look at the opposition Jesus found, and the challenges the disciples faced when they were still fresh from their Pentecost filling with the Spirit.

Don't Run from Refining Fire

There is a refining that takes place in God's way and His will. It was much in evidence in Daniel 3 with Shadrach, Meshach, and Abednego. Here we find three men of integrity and honour. They were not trying to get away with as little commitment as possible. They didn't minimize idolatry and make it acceptable so they wouldn't offend anyone. They were not people-pleasers. This is a simple story that we teach in children's church, but then mostly forget to apply in our own lives. It is an amazing example of how close God is to us when we pass through the refining fire of testing, trouble, and pain.

The Lord was closer to them than their trouble. In fact, they had to go through a literal fire, yet God was with them and never failed them. They were willing to be martyrs and be thrown into a furnace heated at seven times the normal temperature. That kind of courage would not happen overnight. I believe it was made on the anvil of adversity, of testing, and of suffering, and that had produced godliness and integrity. Jesus was so close to them in their time of need. He was with them in the fire. He was with them in the time of refining. God is good and never leaves us to get by alone.

If you are like me, when I go through tough or testing times, I feel the grip of fear coming to overwhelm me. When God is with us in the refining fire, we find foreboding and trepidation replaced by joy and peace. The amazing fifteenth-century reformer John Huss said just before he was burned at the stake for his faith, "Most joyfully will I confirm with my blood that truth which I have written and preached." The refiner's fire is not meant to push the panic button in us; it is meant to push the joy button.

When we find ourselves in troubles, loss, sorrow, trials, and difficulties, the great temptation is to run from the refining process, yet the truth is that the presence of God in the fire can do the impossible and take you into joy. As Nehemiah declared during the time of testing: "The joy of the Lord is your strength" (Nehemiah 8:10). Let the joy of the Lord fill you in the fire. It feels extremely counter-intuitive, but isn't that just like the kingdom of God? We overcome not because we are strong, but because we are weak, which is where His strength is made perfect.

The Bible is packed with such testimonies. Look at the trials faced by Joseph in the latter chapters of Genesis. He was sold into slavery and left for dead by his brothers. He was falsely accused and spent years in prison through a miscarriage of justice. He could have spent his time wallowing in rejection or self-pity, or protesting his rights, but the truth was that the Lord was preparing Him for leadership. God took that young man, refined him, and brought forth silver and gold.

I remember hearing a testimony from a businessman who had been through what to him felt like a refining fire in the recession of the 1990s. His small business nearly went under and he would go into the shop each day and get on his knees to ask the Lord for the money to pay the salaries. This was a time of testing, struggle, and trouble, but he was on his knees as a Christian businessman. He told me how the Lord had given him Psalm 13 to pray. This is a brutally honest psalm. The writer clearly felt forgotten at times. He felt as though God was hiding from him, and there was a wrestling with sorrow and a sense of being overcome. My friend clearly identified with the psalmist. Verse 1 laments, "How long, Lord? Will you forget me for ever?" I think many people might feel they resonate with that verse at times. Yet it is the final verse (verse 6) that holds the key to joy and breakthrough;

But I trust in your unfailing love;
my heart rejoices in your salvation.
I will sing the Lord's praise,
for he has been good to me.

When life seems at its worst and the refiner's fire seems seven times hotter than normal, "But I trust ... my heart rejoices ... I will sing ... he has been good to me." My friend's business did not go under during that recession, but he did pass through the refiner's fire, producing gold and silver as he put God first.

When Brother Yun taught in our church, one line from his testimony really stood out for me. Jesus appeared to him and told him to get up and walk out of the prison where he was being held because of his faith in Jesus. Brother Yun protested and reminded Jesus that his legs were broken and this was a maximum-security prison. Brother Yun said that Jesus spoke to him these words: "This prison is real, but I am the truth." God meets people in their need. The refiner's fire is His instrument of meeting us in His kindness, and of changing us to be more like Him.

The fire of God brings a precious refining. It is God's instrument of blessing in our lives. Sometimes the refiner's fire is the conduit for the revival fire, both personally and as a community. In fact, as difficult as it seems, we need the refining fire, so we must not run from it. During times of testing, trials, troubles, and difficulties we often ask the Lord to remove them and give us a break. We would prefer not to pass through the refiner's fire. We would rather comfort and ease. The refining fire never comes at a convenient moment for us. We would love an exemption, but please don't run from refining; rather let the Lord fully complete His work in you. We know the Christian life is not easy, but the Lord is kind and loving in His refining.

When Caroline and I got married, I got a job with a fantastic UK-based mission agency that worked all over the world. It was my dream job, working with short-term mission volunteers. We had seen it as a sign of God's provision for us as a newly married couple. But six months in, the job came to an end. I found this a very difficult experience. I remember going home and talking with Caroline. It had been totally unexpected. We had many questions, and the fear of where our income would come from was near the top of the list. Together we went into the process of the refiner's fire. It is in situations like this that we are tempted to panic and give in to fear.

I remember we took a walk around Christchurch meadow in Oxford. We talked and prayed, and by the end of our walk we were strangely excited because of the new challenge. We really felt the grace of God that afternoon. He met us in the trial of impending unemployment and gave us a fresh vision as we gave the situation to Him.

Leaning into impossibilities is something God calls us to do. We had to walk this out day by day, but amazingly, within the following three months, the decision was unexpectedly reversed and my contract was renewed. Praise God. I know that even if it hadn't been, God was with us in the fire. He always responds to faithfulness in times of testing.

The refiner's fire has many faces: chronic sickness, pain, loss, bereavement, unemployment, distress, pressure, trauma, suffering, and worry. The list could go on and on, with a complex array of issues that we feel could easily defeat us. Troubles can come into our every waking thought, but the Lord is closer. He is nearer than our trials and temptations. Our wilderness is His workplace. Will we stop running away from the refiner's fire and start leaning into God so that we may find His joy and peace?

Strangely, I think being outside refining is more dangerous for us. Think about it. Without the refiner's fire we are more easily drawn into independence, mediocrity, and self-sufficiency. Worldly comfort tends to lead us away from Christlikeness. Fire leads us to our knees, where the Lord shows us His ways and character. As the apostle Paul declared, "I want to know Christ – yes, to know the power of his resurrection and participation in his sufferings, becoming like him in his death, and so, somehow, attaining to the resurrection from the dead" (Philippians 3:10). Jesus is with us in the fire, and we can encounter Him more than we might realize in times of trouble.

God's Glory and Fiery Trials

The Bible is very open about suffering for being a Christian. It was something that many early Christians across the early church experienced. In Jesus' teaching there was a very clear theme of expectation of persecution.[21] Persecution was a key part of the story of Acts, and in fact it was one of the main reasons for the dispersion of the early church and spread of the gospel. Paul was no stranger to persecution. He had formerly been a persecutor of the church and then went on to suffer for Christ (2 Timothy 3:12, 2 Corinthians 4:8–12, and Philippians 1:12–14).

As Paul shares his own fiery trials, he brings out a theme that is often attached to teaching on persecution. He writes in Philippians 1:12 that his suffering "served to advance the gospel". This kind of teaching is found all over the Bible when persecution or fiery trials are discussed. Jesus made incredible promises to those who were persecuted, such as in Matthew 5:10: "Blessed are those who are persecuted because of righteousness, for theirs is the kingdom of heaven." It seems that there is always an encouragement, a promise, or an assurance of God's reward and empowering or a greater sense of bringing God glory through remaining faithful.

21 See Mark 13:11–13, John 15:18–25, Matthew 5:10, and Luke 6:22 for just a few examples.

This New Testament theme comes out very strongly in 1 Peter. He writes of trials, "These have come so that the proven genuineness of your faith – of greater worth than gold, which perishes even through refined by fire – may result in praise, glory and honour when Jesus Christ is revealed" (1 Peter 1:7). Peter was letting the Christians of Asia Minor know that they would suffer all kinds of trials for the name of Jesus. Again, though, along with the fact of persecution came the purpose. It would result in praise, glory, and honour for Jesus. Just as with Shadrach, Meshach, and Abednego, God would be glorified through their faithfulness, no matter what the adversity.

This seems perhaps a strange concept to us. We tend to think of God being glorified though less costly means. We don't really consider exalting God in our suffering, yet it is clear in both Scripture and church history throughout the ages that fiery trials result in glory to God as His people remain faithful. Far from being unusual, it seems to have been considered an integral part of Christian experience in Scripture and history. If you read accounts of trials in the persecuted church today, you will find that they are not pressing for their rights to be upheld; the people are simply seeking to be like Jesus and praying for their enemies, loving them and seeking to win them to Christ. This is the kind of story that brings glory to God.

Try exalting God in suffering. This is what it looks like to be on fire for God. Try praising Him in all circumstances. Perhaps we would learn to see our circumstances through the eyes of faith, not fear. Maybe then we would see opportunities for grace and the gospel in all of life's circumstances. Is passionate worship only for the happy times? Are we Christians only when life is good? Let Jesus be glorified through your sorrow, brokenness, unemployment, sickness, or struggle. How is He glorified? God gets the glory through your love and faithfulness through every situation. Blessed be Your name, O Lord!

The refiner's fire burns up self. It is this self-focus that promotes fear, unbelief, and stress. When self is gone, we are free to love and have joy. When we are led to the cross and the love of Jesus, everything is different. The more we focus on ourselves in our trials, the more we go down in despair; but the more we focus on Jesus, thanksgiving will overtake us. The fire helps us fix our eyes on Jesus by burning away self. We must be real and honest in times of trial, but allow the refining fire to be hot enough to burn up self and lead us to Jesus.

Jesus Came to Bring Fire

Jesus is the one we need to stick close to in suffering. Who else could be more than enough for us? Jesus knows our trials. He understands completely. Sometimes people point the finger at God when it comes to suffering, but we have a Saviour who is able to comfort us as One who actually knows the fire of suffering. Being close to Him does not mean the suffering will stop, but it does mean we will know His presence through the fire.

Actually, it is deeper than that. As I reflected on the most famous Bible verse on the refiner's fire in Malachi 3:2, I realized something more profound about Jesus and the refiner's fire.

But who can endure the day of his coming? Who can stand when he appears? For he will be like a refiner's fire or a launderer's soap.

Malachi 3:2

This is a strong Scripture. There is the sense that the refiner's fire is extremely powerful. So much so that no one can stand before it. But the truth revealed here is that the refining fire is not an "it". This fire is God Himself. He is coming, He appears, and He is like a refiner's fire. We can only understand our trials when we know Jesus and are close to Him.

He is like the refiner's fire. This fire is part of His love for us, bringing us into more of His heart of purity and goodness. The refiner's fire burns to purify. God doesn't want alloys in the kingdom. An alloy is a mixture of metals. When it comes to our hearts, God wants no mixture of holiness and selfishness; no double-mindedness. When the fire comes, it separates and brings forth pure gold and silver. So the refiner's fire is not a vague idea or principle. He is the refiner's fire. The fire is a person. Jesus came to bring fire.

Oswald Chambers wrote about this process of refining as the "destruction of every affinity that God has not started".[22] In

22 Chambers, My Utmost for His Highest, p. 27.

the natural world, fire tests and purifies. Its heat purges every impurity. Nothing is safe from intense fire. When I think about my heart, there are many impurities I would love to be purged. What about the lies of the enemy that we believe, the lust of the flesh we entertain, the pride that we harbour, the prejudices that we countenance, and the self-pity in which we indulge? May God come as the refiner's fire to purify, cleanse, and purge every stain and every contamination in my heart. I believe this is what the hymn writer had in mind when these amazing words were penned in the fifteenth century:

Come down, O love divine,
seek thou this soul of mine,
and visit it with thine own ardor glowing;
O Comforter, draw near,
within my heart appear,
and kindle it, thy holy flame bestowing.

O let it freely burn,
till earthly passions turn
to dust and ashes in its heat consuming;
and let thy glorious light
shine ever on my sight,
and clothe me round, the while my path illuming.[23]

This will not be easy or convenient, but He is always good. Heart refining is necessary to reveal the righteousness and

23 Bianco da Siena, "Come Down, O Love Divine", 1434.

glory of God in us. Perhaps the church is too unrefined so we don't see her brightness. Do we desire ease more than fire? Perhaps we keep out of the fire and do all we can not to go there, not realizing that it is the Lord's doing. When God is doing something in your life, don't run away.

I Am Crucified with Christ

I counsel you to buy from me gold refined in the fire, so that you can become rich; and white clothes to wear, so that you can cover your shameful nakedness; and salve to put on your eyes, so that you can see.

Revelation 3:18

Let Jesus be revealed in your testing. The context for this passage on the refiner's fire in Revelation 3 is the recovery of Jesus as your first love. Jesus wants to bring the refiner's fire into the Laodicean church because the church is lukewarm. The greatest gift He could give them would be to refine them. The refiner's fire may be the greatest gift the Lord has for you right at this moment; yet are you trying to run away?

As we have seen, Jesus knows the refiner's fire. He emptied Himself, went to the wilderness, fasted and prayed, and went into poverty and dependence. He went through the pressure of Gethsemane, and the stress caused Him to sweat drops of blood. Then He went willingly to face the agony of the cross where He suffered, even praying, "Father forgive them."

Where did He get that kind of kindness and love? I believe it came through the refiner's fire. When Jesus was under massive pressure and stress, what came out of His heart and mouth? Love, kindness, forgiveness, and goodness. When we are in the crucible, what comes out of our hearts and mouths? Is it anger, bitterness, blame, finger-pointing, resentment, and more? Jesus so humbled and lowered Himself in His downward mobility that God raised Him up. He wants His church to get gold refined in the fire so we can be like Him.

The refiner's fire is God's instrument of personal revival. It is perfectly designed by the Lord for the revealing of His Son through our lives. That is why we need to run towards the fire, not away from it. The refiner's fire says God loves you and wants to display Jesus through you. It always leads to blessing. In Daniel 3 there was the blessing of protection from harm. In Malachi 3 there was the blessing of cleansing. In 1 Peter 1 the blessing came through praise and glory being given to God, and in Revelation 3 Jesus promises that those who "buy" the refined gold from Him will "become rich". These riches are not earthly, but the eternal blessings of knowing and revealing Jesus.

We give so much priority to self-preservation in our thinking and living, but Paul said, "I am crucified with Christ" (Galatians 2:20). Let's not pretend it doesn't hurt. Being crucified is beyond painful. It results in death and there is no turning back. In his book, *The Cost of Discipleship*, Dietrich

Bonhoeffer famously said, "When Christ calls a man, he bids him come and die."[24] But let's also be honest: even when it hurts, we say, "God, I worship you. You are always good. Let Your will, not my will, be done. I am wholly Yours, no matter what." Then we will see a bright church that puts on display Jesus Christ to the nation. It is in dying that we really live. It is in giving that we receive, and it is in being refined by fire that we bring God glory and will become eternally rich.

24 Dietrich Bonhoeffer, *The Cost of Discipleship*, London: SCM Press, 1948/2001, p. 44.

Chapter 6

Set Ablaze by Love

Place me like a seal over your heart,
like a seal on your arm;
for love is as strong as death,
its jealousy unyielding as the grave.
It burns like blazing fire,
like a mighty flame.

Song of Songs 8:6

This is a truth very close to my heart. I wish I could adequately convey to you my deep longing for intimacy with God. I am very much on a journey in prayer and, like so many, I have so much to learn of the disciplines of intimacy. But I know that my heart aches for God, for more of His presence, for more of His nearness, and for His beauty and perfect love to fill every part of my heart and life.

This hunger for God's intimate presence was first awakened as I discovered and experienced His awesome closeness and the sense that He was actually and personally there with me during prayer, worship, and Bible reading. His intimate presence became a reality to me that was so much more than just knowing my Bible. It was a real soul communion with God. To see with my heart even faint glimpses of Jesus was all it took, and I longed for more. Honestly, I still long for more.

My life's struggle is to hush the competing distractions of this life that seek to drown my soul hunger for intimacy with my heavenly Father. I have a quiet, inner knowledge that I was made for intimacy with God. But when I consider the mighty love God has for me, why do I so struggle to know how to be intimately connected with Him in return? I believe this struggle is familiar to many Christians.

For many years as a Christian I had no idea of the depth of relationship that God intended for me. I was aware of Jesus as Saviour and Lord, but less aware of Him as closest friend or the heavenly Bridegroom. The idea of loving God was basically translated as being thankful to Him for dying on the cross, but there was no actual sense of intimacy, personal relationship, or nearness to His heart. As I heard Christians pray, there was reverence and respect, but conversations with God never sounded anything like an intimate relationship. God still seemed very much in heaven and we were very much on earth. There were no role models who seemed to know God like that.

Let me ask this question: why is it so rare to meet people who are on fire with this passionate love for God? I meet so many Christians who struggle with the basic sense of lack of deep connection with God. Is it that we don't really value intimacy with God enough? Maybe we have never thought about God in that way? Maybe we leave it to others or don't have the time to develop the relationship? More and more people have a longing to go deeper with God, and yet intimacy with Him is still either simply underestimated or seen as unattainable. Many of us are activists who love to organize church, lead programmes, and host events, but are we hungry for Him? I find in myself a frustrating mixture of the contemplative and the activist. Does anyone else feel like both Mary and Martha put together (Luke 10:38–42)? I love to sit and listen to Him and also to be His servant about His business.

One thing I know is that there is a clear and profound connection between God's holy fire and the revelation and experience of His love. God is calling us to intimacy as a key to bringing and sustaining revival. Blazing fire is a powerful symbol of passionate love. I believe perhaps the highest expression of the fire of God is in experiencing the fire of His love. Even using the language of being "on fire for God" is shorthand for passionately loving God. Being on fire is really about being set ablaze by His love.

So how do we get into the place of such fiery intimacy? The answer seems too simple because we think we know it already, but in reality we have not yet begun to explore its many-splendoured depths and power. The answer is in personally knowing and relying on the fiery love of God. There are no shortcuts here. We need it to be more normal to meet people who are mature in intimacy with God, who really know God deeply and love Him fervently.

So what does it look like to love God? What does intimacy with God involve? If we are honest, many of us simply don't know because we have never seen someone relate to God at that level of nearness. Seeking an answer here has made me begin to see discipleship differently. I would love to see us not just teaching on prayer classroom style, but how about getting on our knees together and learning together how to draw close to God. We need the kind of discipleship that is not just about information but is also about apprenticing people in the kingdom and getting into prayer, the Word, and worship together so that we may learn to get through to God in prayer. Discipleship is not a course; it is a lifestyle, and that is how we need to learn this intimacy with God. We learn together as disciples. What an adventure this could be for a small group, to really learn to pray and connect with God in a deeper way than ever before.

Leaning on the Beloved

One of the best places to begin to answer what intimacy with God is like is in the Song of Songs. This incredible scriptural love poem is very intimate. As we bring it into our New Testament understanding in the light of Jesus, we can interpret the book as a picture or type of the relationship between Jesus and His people, the church. This interpretation is commonly held today among many church leaders and theologians. It is an allegory for what it looks and feels like to love God, having first experienced His love. I would strongly recommend doing more reading and reflecting on the Song of Songs. I have benefited from the insights of writers such as Watchman Nee, Mike Bickle, and C. H. Spurgeon. There are many powerful images in this divine love poem.

Let's take a look at the amazing verses in Song of Songs 8:5–6. What a description of strong, unyielding and intimate love. Just preceding this powerful statement on what fiery love looks like, we see a beautiful picture of the Lover leaning on her Beloved. Verse 5 starts with a question from the friends: "Who is this coming up from the wilderness leaning upon her beloved?" The person leaning represents the Lover, which can be interpreted as the church, and the Beloved is interpreted as Jesus, the Bridegroom. The friends are slightly bemused onlookers who don't seem to understand the full extent of the love between the Lover and the Beloved. There are many onlookers like them in the church today. When it comes to passion for God, they just don't get it, but they are intrigued.

I first encountered this Scripture through a prophetic word the Lord gave to me during a tough time of personal anxiety about my health. As I was praying one day, I felt I simply heard the Lord whisper to my soul, "Lean on the Beloved." This word gave me real comfort. I held on to it as a word from the Lord and it stayed in my heart as a beautiful picture of how God wanted me to draw close to Him in times of trouble. The Lord gave me the phrase before I even knew it was in the Bible. You can imagine my surprise and delight when one day I discovered it in Song of Songs 8:5.

Notice that the Lover is coming up from the wilderness, leaning on the Beloved. The wilderness is the place of struggle and weakness. Jesus' ministry was launched in the wilderness when He was hungry and dependent on His Father. Intimacy with God is for people who feel like they are struggling, people who feel weak and don't have it all together. It isn't for those who are strong in their own strength. We are invited into this intimacy in our weakness and wilderness. You can know the nearness of Jesus in the middle of your brokenness. We don't have to be all sorted or perfect to be close to God. I love the picture of leaning on the Beloved. There is such a sense of nearness, intensity, depth, closeness, warmth, confidence, and understanding. Leaning speaks primarily to me about trusting. We lean on Him and, although we are weak, He is strong.

Love Like Blazing Fire

Now look at verses 6 and 7, where the strength of fiery love is expressed in the strongest possible terms by the Lover. There is nothing average or mediocre about this love. As we interpret it for our time, it is a prayer that our love for Christ would be like a blazing fire and a mighty flame. Do we allow the love of God to be such a powerful force in our souls? Do we pray with this intensity? Jesus wants our hearts to be wholly for Him. Jesus wants us to be blazing hot (Revelation 3:15–16). The prayer to be placed like a seal on His arm was a reference to being a bond-slave, a sign that we freely belong to Him.

Passion is sometimes uncomfortable to onlookers. It makes us feel uneasy in our mediocre world that likes to mock fervour. What kind of response do you think our God deserves from us? Are we onlookers or lovers? Are we consumers or disciples? It's time for more genuine and audacious passion in the church for the magnificent name of Jesus. This is what fuels mission, worship, prayer, and sacrificial love for others. We love Him because He first loved us. He has utterly won our hearts. Are we fit to burst with His love?

If you think the love expressed through Song of Songs sets a high standard, it becomes even stronger in the writings of the apostle John. Every Christian should know John 17:26. The implications for this verse, let alone the whole chapter, are staggering. John records Jesus' words as He prays: "I have made you known to them, and will continue to make you known in order that the love you have for me may be in them and that I myself may be in them." Jesus prayed that the strength and quality of love between the Father and Son would also be between Him and us. Did you get that? Jesus prayed that we might experience the same kind of love that flows within the Trinity. It doesn't get any more powerful than that.

Fire in His Eyes

The book of Song of Songs has many parallels in the New Testament. The same message of love certainly shines through John's gospel and epistles. Another place where similar imagery is used is in the book of Revelation, also written by the apostle John. Every time I read Revelation I feel I get a glimpse of eternity. I particularly love reading of the scenes around the throne room in heaven and the glorious descriptions of the Lord Jesus in His risen and ascended majesty.

People sometimes read Revelation looking for complex "end-time theories". This is fine, except that the main purpose of the book is stated in the first verse as "the revelation of Jesus Christ" (NIV 1984). This is the crying need today: a transforming revelation of the person of the Lord Jesus Christ. As we read about Jesus in Revelation we discover a phrase that we will remember from Song of Songs 8:6. Three times we have this description of the eyes of Jesus as blazing fire.

The hair on his head was white like wool, as white as snow, and his eyes were like blazing fire.

Revelation 1:14

To the angel of the church in Thyatira write:
These are the words of the Son of God, whose eyes are like blazing fire and whose feet are like burnished bronze.

Revelation 2:18

His eyes are like blazing fire, and on his head are many crowns. He has a name written on him that no one knows but he himself.

Revelation 19:12

This is just my own prayerful understanding, because I am aware that the blazing fire communicates so much more than intimacy; but I believe it is true that the description of Jesus' eyes of blazing fire in Revelation can be interpreted as His passionate love for His people. Jesus looks at His church with the eyes of blazing fire. I believe this is a description of fiery intimacy and love. He looks at us with eyes of holiness, purity, and love. When we look into someone's eye we look into their soul. What does John see? Blazing fire. God loves us with a blazing fire. His eyes are upon us.

Jesus wants us to see His burning eyes. When we know someone, we look into their eyes. Looking someone in the eye is key to friendship, intimacy, and trust. Even one glimpse of those fiery eyes of the Lord Jesus Christ would cure so much of our compromise. One holy glance from Him would change our lives. Are we willing to gaze into those eyes of fire? Are we ready to come face to face with God? These moments of gazing on Jesus are life-transforming.

I believe the fire of God is centred on Jesus. His fire brings judgment, purity, refining, holiness, and the power of the Spirit, but supremely, it is all about knowing the Lord Jesus Christ. Jesus meant for us to know that His eyes are blazing fire. When we read His word, spend time with Him in prayer, honour Him in worship, or serve Him among the poor, we can see those blazing eyes of fiery love and goodness.

Sean Fuecht and Andy Byrd describe this:

Our desire is to behold His glory and receive the passion in His heart. It is the same passion that took Him to the cross, the passion that conquered the grave, and the passion that will bring Him back to His glorious Bride at the end of the age for the wedding supper of the Lamb. Face to face intimacy! The fire in His eyes will spread to our hearts and begin to burn up the chaff that competes for our attention and affections. As the chaff is burned up, what remains is a heart, mind and life completely devoted to Him as Lord."[25]

Knowing that Jesus looks at you with eyes of blazing fire, what is your response? Jesus came to impart His fire to us. Given His blazing eyes, how can we remain lukewarm? For me, the goal of prayer, praise, and serving others is to see Jesus.

You Can't Mature Beyond Love

Sadly, some Christians dismiss the importance of experiencing the love of God. Perhaps they see it as too sentimental. I have heard and read some leaders describe this teaching on love as making the church too feminine. Do men really want to sing worship songs about loving God? They seem to suggest that this is why men don't like church. I have to say that I see it completely differently. Intimately worshipping God whose

25 Sean Fuecht and Andy Byrd, *Fire and Fragrance*, Destiny Image, 2010, p. 211.

love led Him to die for us does not put our masculinity at risk in any way. I believe men are drawn to intimacy with God.

I can't honestly think of any higher or more mature expression of doctrine than to continue to explore the love of God for eternity and then still not to have exhausted its limitless depths. You can't mature beyond the cross or the love that took Jesus there for us. While we were His enemies in sin and deserved the fire of hell, Jesus came from heaven to save us. The Bible clearly says that "God is love" (1 John 4:8).

There is nothing deeper than God's love. Ephesians 3:17–19 makes that point very clearly:

> And I pray that you, being rooted and established in
> love, may have power, together with all the Lord's holy
> people, to grasp how wide and long and high and deep
> is the love of Christ, and to know this love that surpasses
> knowledge – that you may be filled to the measure of all
> the fullness of God.

God's love is inexhaustible, incomparable, and incredible. It is a lavish love that has no upper limit. You can go as far as you like in God's love. There is always more and always enough. Whenever we encounter the fire of God, it is always an encounter with love. The refiner's fire only makes sense through love. The wrath of God only makes sense when we see His love. The holiness of God is fundamentally an expression of His love. Everything about God needs to be seen through the glorious height, length, and depth of the fullness of a love that passes knowledge. When we encounter God, we encounter His love.

The whole story of redemption is a love story. The first Adam went to sleep and the Lord brought a bride from his side. The second Adam (Jesus) went to death and the Lord brought a bride (the church) from His wounded side (Romans 5:12–21). Jesus came from eternity into time with blazing love. His story is a love story. "God so loved the world that he gave his one and only Son" (John 3:16). At the cross, as our sin and shame are defeated, we can see most perfectly that full extent of God's love for us. What amazing love! Jesus deserves praise, glory, and all our worship as the One who has covered our sin, through His precious blood, shed because of such love.

First Commandment First

Jesus left us in no doubt about the priority of love. In Mark 12:28–34 we can see clearly what Jesus considers to be important:

> "'Hear, O Israel: the Lord our God, the Lord is one. Love the Lord your God with all your heart and with all your soul and with all your mind and with all your strength.' The second is this: 'Love your neighbour as yourself.' There is no commandment greater than these."

What would our lives look like if we put the first commandment first? This is what it means to love Jesus. This comes with priority over our careers, home improvements, TV habits, leisure time, and even families. Love God first, others and ourselves second. I once heard the preacher Todd White put it well: he said that unless we love God most, we won't be able to love others more.

I want to be as clear as I can be on this. The church suffers today from the major problem that Christians often see themselves, not God, as the centre of the relationship. This is not what Jesus taught. Jesus believed in loving ourselves, but only in the context of loving God first and loving others as much as we love ourselves. This is radical in our self-centred and individualistic culture.

When we think of commandments, we tend to remember Moses and the Ten Commandments written on stone. We think of the law and don't often associate Jesus with giving commandments, but He did. Jesus gave lots of commandments to us. These are not lived through the law to gain salvation, but in the power of the Holy Spirit from the place of being saved through Jesus and seeking to live for the kingdom of God. In John 14:15, Jesus says, "If you love me, keep my commands." In fact, there are something like thirty-eight commandments given by Jesus in the four gospels. Again, these are not given for our salvation, which comes through the cross and resurrection, but they are given to enable us to learn to walk with God. Let me remind you of just some of them:

- "Go and make disciples of all nations." (Matthew 28:19)
- "Be merciful, just as your Father is merciful." (Luke 6:36)
- "You also should wash one another's feet." (John 13:14)
- "You must be born again." (John 3:7)
- "Watch out for false prophets." (Matthew 7:15)
- "Ask … seek … knock." (Matthew 7:7)
- "Do not judge." (Matthew 7:1)
- "Seek first his kingdom and his righteousness." (Matthew 6:33)
- "Do not worry about your life." (Matthew 6:25)
- "Love your enemies." (Matthew 5:44)

Let's briefly unpack this greatest commandment some more. Jesus calls us to love God with heart, soul, mind, and strength.

Heart – The Bible has much to say about the human heart. It seems to represent our inner life. It is the seat of our emotions. Loving God with all our heart speaks of wholeheartedness, commitment, passion, and zeal. We must not be afraid to love God with all our heart.

Soul – I believe loving God with all our soul has something to do with making sure our true identity is in relationship with Jesus rather than with the world. This is about being rooted and established in love. This is powerful in an insecure, fearful, anxious world. Knowing God's love makes us secure.

Mind – The mind is a spiritual battleground where Jesus wants to bring victory. It is a doorway to the inner man. In Romans 12:1-2 is a call to be transformed through the renewed mind. Loving God with all our mind means thinking like Jesus.

Strength – This is a call for us to place the love of God at the centre of our productivity. We can only be fruitful in His love. Our work and purpose for life come through His love. Make every action, no matter how menial or purposeful, an act of love for His glory, and God will release blessing.

When we love God like this, there is no capacity for other loves. The greatest commandment may seem like a tall order. But at its heart it is very simple: love God and then love others and yourself. There is something about the order that flows first to God that means we are able to fulfil the second commandment with much greater effect. We must keep the order as Jesus commanded. Loving Him brings heaven's resources to love others and indeed to love ourselves.

Do You Love Me?

Jesus never stopped loving, no matter what happened to Him. He just kept on loving. Jesus' love is cross love, tough love, passionate love, jealous love, holy love, pure love. The total abandonment of the cross will always serve to remind us that He literally loves us completely, holding nothing back.

But then, in response to His love, do I live like I love Jesus? Does my relationship with Jesus take priority in my life, and can it be evidenced in my daily lifestyle? Intimacy with God puts Jesus at the centre of the relationship. If my life is full of selfishness, then perhaps I need to get on my knees and get right with God, so I can live with Him more at the centre and find the blessing of His nearness and presence.

This is something we see happening in Peter's life, and he had a conversation with Jesus in John 21:15–17. Peter had failed Jesus in His time of need. Peter's denial of Jesus showed the true depth of his relationship with Him, and Peter's own fears had won the day. This was deeply painful for Peter, and so Jesus led Him through a process of restoration and healing that would have an impact on his life for evermore.

Jesus wanted to draw out the priority of intimacy with the question to Peter, "Do you love me more than these?" No one really knows what the "these" Jesus referred to were, but the point remains that Jesus was lovingly restoring Peter. As we consider this conversation today, we might well hear Jesus say:

Do you love me more than your family?
Do you love me more than your money?
Do you love me more than your reputation?
Do you love me more than your home and possessions?
Do you love me more than your dreams and plans?

Jesus asked Peter three times if he loved Him. Peter replied each time with increasing desperation and ended up feeling hurt. Jesus then reinstated Peter by saying, "Follow me!" (verse 19). I believe it is time we resolved our lack of deep connection and intimate relationship with Jesus. Do we love Him?

This strong connection of love for God is also the best way to love one another. It is a prerequisite for loving one another in the first commandment. Loving God makes loving one another not only possible but also powerful. We all long for deeper connection with one another and for friendships and relationships that go deeper. The way to love one another more is to love God first.

God's fire and love go together. If we want our love to be renewed, we need to ask God to light the fire in our hearts again. The fire of intimacy with Jesus is the answer to the lost connection. Perhaps it is time to get on your knees before God, to cry out to know His love, and to give Him your love as never before. "Father, come and light the fire of blazing love in me."

Chapter 7

Don't Fight the Fire

*The Lord spoke to you face to face out of the fire on the
mountain. (At that time I stood between the Lord and you to
declare to you the word of the Lord, because you were afraid
of the fire and did not go up the mountain.)*

Deuteronomy 5:4–5

A s I look across the church scene in the United
Kingdom, I feel a real sense of sorrowful concern.
Why is there so little fire? Please don't get me wrong;
I love the church deeply. I believe the church as the bride of
Christ is destined to reflect His glory, but that is where my
sadness lies: she is not reflecting His glory in the way she
could. Something has made the church grow cold.

Rather than love, service, and passion, we see too much
compromise, division, and dullness for her to be the bride and
body of Christ that we know the church really is called to be.
Right now, as a whole, we are not representing Jesus well to
our communities and nation. What is troubling is that it does
not have to be this way. We seem to have chosen to quench the
fire of God rather than to fan it into flame. We have become
expert firefighters.

I want to go on record with my deep conviction that I believe and pray that we are going to see the largest and most powerful revival the UK has ever seen and that the church and nation will be transformed by the grace of God. That is what I am living and leading for. I believe that is God's heart: to pour out His Spirit upon all people. But right now, if we are honest, we are not in great shape as church in the UK. Yes, there are some wonderful encouragements and great testimonies of healings and blessings, but as a whole the nation continues to be disengaged and the church is in slow retreat in so many places. Over 95 per cent of the population is not planning on worshipping with us around the country next weekend.

It is true that the Church of England has seen tremendous progress and change over the past thirty years, and more Spirit-filled leaders are now entering ordained ministry than ever. However, there is also a trend towards a loss of confidence in biblical authority and teaching, even in churches that would describe themselves as evangelical and charismatic. Christian leaders are fearful to take a stand on a number of countercultural issues such as a positive biblical view of sex and marriage, and Jesus as the only way to salvation. The prayer meeting continues to be the Cinderella of the church – unloved and overlooked. Why is this so? Where have we gone wrong? How can we put things right?

I believe the answer is in recovering the fire of God in our lives and churches. The message of fire is not new. It is an ancient solution to our contemporary problems. Have we been fighting God's fire? Perhaps we have become firefighters instead of fire-starters?

I love the words of William Booth, founder of the Salvation Army. In a hymn composed in 1894 he wrote, "The fire will meet our every need." He wrote of beginning a revolution of the fire of God bringing holiness, light, and courage into the church.[26] We need to recover His fire. The fire is so precious and indispensable to the church. To renew the fire is to restore His holiness, presence, and love.

Why have we allowed the magnificent, intimate, and powerful love of Christ to leaves us cold, passive, and unmoved? Why don't we get more stirred up? Why are we not more on fire with this love? I hope you can hear that my heart is not to condemn but to encourage us and call us into a renewed place of fiery, authentic, real, powerful Christian experience and faith. We have settled for something too pale that does not reflect the true and living God who created heaven and earth and who is awesome in His holy love and power. There is so much more than we are currently seeing and experiencing. I want us to throw off the wishy-washy, colourless, comatose brand of Christianity that has kept us comfy, but not holy. We were born again for more than this.

26 William Booth, "Send the Fire", 1894.

We are Afraid of the Fire

This frosty condition of God's people is not new. In Deuteronomy 5:4–5 we read that even though the blessing of face-to-face communion with God was available to the people and His presence was manifest to them on the mountain, the people were afraid and so missed out on knowing God. They missed God's blessing!

Could it be that we are very like those Israelites and that we are in our predicament today because we, too, are afraid of the fire? Afraid because we don't know how to be with God and how to relate to God, so we have chosen to remain at a distance, and therein lies our defeat. In a way, we want to be kept safe from the heavenly fire. We don't want it. We are fighting and quenching the fire to keep us safe, shielded, and defended from too much of God. We are afraid of what might happen should fire break out.

If we recognize this fear, then it is worth reflecting on why we are afraid. Where has it come from, and what might it be like to live in freedom from it? I believe most Christians want to love God with more passion and to see more of His kingdom come in their lives, but they would also recognize that there are powerful fears that hold them back. Let's be honest in our reflections: what is this fear about? Why are we afraid? Maybe then we can progress more fruitfully in our repentance and see the stronghold of fear broken.

I have considered this fear and have identified four ways in which it reaches into our lives to fight the fire of God in us. I see them all in myself, and I recognize the fierce battle to go forward.

It feels like taking a step into the unknown

Most Christians want to live for God, but it can just seem too intense to be totally surrendered to God because we don't know what it looks like and we don't like change. It can feel like stepping into the unknown. What will it mean for me? How will life change? What will I have to do or give up? There are so many questions and complications that we find it easier to withdraw and stay in the background rather than to step out spiritually.

I am conscious that there will be people who will read this entire book and agree with much of what it says, but will feel paralysed about what to do with it. I have often felt this way myself. I recently reread my journal from 2004 and read my heart's cry, "I don't know how to be with you, Lord. Help me." I was frustrated, disappointed, and insecure. I think it stems from not necessarily seeing examples of people in our churches to whom we can relate who are on fire for God, with whom we can journey and from whom we can learn. No one is going to tick all the boxes and get everything right. We learn through failures, setbacks, and persevering through struggles, and it is much easier to do this alongside others, especially if they are mature believers. I would love to see more people coming together in discipleship communities to seek to live together on fire for God.

So it could be about not having a model for what it looks like to be on fire, but I also think something else is going on in this mindset. Really, this is about a fear of the future and about losing control. In large and small ways we quite enjoy being masters of our own destiny, and this desire to control quenches all risk or prospect of being radical. We are glad that others are being radical and we have read their missionary biographies, and for some reason we applaud but do not emulate them.

It has to do with control. Who is in control in your life? I believe this is also of importance when it comes to the fullness of the Holy Spirit. Many Christians know about the Holy Spirit, but they would prefer to be measured and controlled and so they have not surrendered to the Spirit.

In dealing with this fear, I see freedom coming through the truth of the Lordship of Christ over our lives. In short, becoming a Christian is to surrender to Christ. When we came to Christ at the beginning of our Christian experience, we came to Him as Saviour and Lord. He is Lord of all. The Christian life is a step into the unknown with Jesus. This has always been true, even for the first disciples. Jesus called them to "Follow me", and they left everything to follow Him. The life on fire for God is really no different to the implications of the gospel upon every Christian. This is how it is supposed to be. Really, there ought not to be a Christian who is described as on fire for God. Being on fire is integral to what it means to be a Christian.

What will others think?

Fear of others' opinions is a big fire-quencher. The Bible says in Proverbs 29:25 that, "Fear of man will prove to be a snare." But people often forget to quote the second part of the sentence. The full verse says, "Fear of man will prove to be a snare, but whoever trusts in the Lord is kept safe." True security is found in trusting in the Lord.

We worry about what others will think if we get too passionate or committed to Christ. Do you think it is possible to be over-committed to Christ? Given His total self-giving for us on the cross, could I ever be in danger of being too committed to Him? Still, I have always found that my spiritual temperature cools significantly when I am bound by the fear of man. This fear is evidenced when people struggle even to worship freely or pray aloud for fear that we will draw attention to ourselves or get something wrong. How we need to be set free from this fear. It throws cold water over sparks of prayer and worship. May God give us courage to pray, worship, and witness with genuine wholeheartedness, holding nothing back.

Many people fear not being able to keep renewed spiritual passion going. How many times have I sought to renew a spiritual discipline and within two weeks have found myself back where I started? Surely I will lose face when people see that nothing has changed. This fear is often most pronounced in the home, because our families know us for who we really are. Even within marriages, many husbands and wives struggle to pray together because it is so intimate and makes us feel vulnerable.

I believe the antidote to the fear of man is the fear of God. The fear of God is not based on performance, but on love. Proverbs 9:10 declares, "The fear of the Lord is the beginning of wisdom." This godly fear places God's honour above fear of what anyone else may think or concern for our own reputation or embarrassment. The fear of the Lord says, "I am not ashamed of the gospel" (Romans 1:16). It places Jesus above all, dies to self, and is fully alive with worship and adoration. It is a mindset that believes that all that really matters is what God thinks of me. The fear of the Lord gives such security as my identity comes from Him, not from how people see me.

It will mean sacrifice and surrender

The fear of loss is perhaps one of the biggest reasons why people choose distance from God. We spend our lives gathering wealth, working to provide homes and comforts, and trying our best to make ourselves secure in this life, and we cannot countenance any threat to the way of life to which we have aspired and become accustomed. We have forgotten that true comfort comes from our Creator and Saviour.

Jesus tackled this fear head-on many times. One such incident comes in Matthew 19:16–24 with the rich young ruler who came with enthusiasm to Jesus, but left sorrowful because he could not imagine making such sacrifices. He chose earthly wealth rather than building treasure in heaven. How do you interpret Matthew 19:16–24?

What is the normal Christian life? In the Western church we are much like the world around us, finding ourselves confused because there seem to be so many ways to answer the questions about how we should live our lives. This confusion has created a "pick 'n' mix" philosophy, which means our highest value is being able to choose from a variety of sources how I want to live. Self is at the centre. We muddle through life with good intentions, but often feel that there is no real anchor to our lives; we never quite feel assured that what we are doing is right or really satisfies. We need an anchor for our souls.

I know many people feel they have a limited capacity to live life that is increasingly complex and tiring. People have busy jobs, full weekends, and multilayered demands of various types of family life. Many people feel that they are already running on empty and that a call to live more on fire for God is just another thing to make them worn out. I think there can be a huge fear of over-committing to church or to God. Is it any wonder in this high-speed culture that people have lost their cutting edge? No one benefits from being rushed, and it only leads to hard-heartedness. The lifestyle of "fitting God in" knows no fire.

I believe the normal Christian life is about sacrifice, servanthood, and sharing. Jesus never promised that we would be comfortable or wealthy. He promised fullness of life, joy, peace, hope, and blessing, and He said it would mean sacrifice, suffering, and persecution along the way. Jesus' teaching prepared His disciples to expect trouble from the world. Look at John 15:20 where Jesus told His disciples to expect persecution because no servant is greater than his master. Look at the kind of church described in Acts. It was a church full of love, fellowship, signs, wonders and miracles, and also persecution. We don't need safety as much as we need the fire of God.

I was recently profoundly challenged reading about a pastor from the Chinese church who wrote these words from prison:

> *Suffering challenges so many people in the world.*
> *Without suffering how is it possible to taste the depths of*
> *the goodness of the Lord? After tasting of it, how can one*
> *be obsessed with worldly desires? Oh Suffering, I used*
> *to flee from you. But today the Lord has commanded*
> *me to endure all you have for me. Oh Suffering, did*
> *not the apostles welcome you? Oh Suffering, you make*
> *my moments with the Lord so much better. You are*
> *the oxygen of the saints. Without you they would have*
> *stopped breathing.*[27]

27 For the entire poem, see E. Bach, *Back to Jerusalem: 30 Day Devotional*, Back to Jerusalem, pp. 17–18.

How do we respond? All we can do is as simply and honestly as we can, say "Yes" to Jesus and all He calls us to. We do need to count the cost, and I pray that we will be willing to go through with God whatever the cost may be. Jesus called us to take up our cross daily with Him. I don't say this lightly, but I do believe this is where real joy and peace are found. We make it so complicated, but Jesus didn't. It is really about childlike trust and obedience to our Heavenly Father based on His sacrifice, not ours.

I am not good enough

This is one I battle with all the time. I battle with them all, but this feels like a daily battle. The fear of failure so hinders us in our journey with God. How many of us battle with a strong sense of insignificance and inadequacy? We feel we don't know enough, don't pray enough, don't know the Scriptures as we feel we should, and on it goes. I remember an amazing member of our church family once said that for many years he just never felt good enough.

Sadly, this is a seed sown by many Christian leaders who are constantly keeping up pressure on people to be better Christians; people feel oppressed by never being good enough, no matter what they do. It is not hard to find Christians who feel crushed, powerless, immobilized, and purposeless. No wonder people in this mindset simply feel flattened by thinking about the fire of God. It compounds their stronghold even further.

This insignificance stronghold is a lie that is designed to knock us out of the battle by taming our spiritual authority and focusing us on ourselves, rather than on the grace of God. The truth is that in Christ we have been given power and authority to bring the kingdom of God into every circumstance (Luke 9:1). It is not that we are good enough, but that God's grace is enough. God's unmerited favour is extended to us. His empowering presence is not based on our goodness, but upon His grace. We will never be good enough in our own strength, but we can do all things through Him. Have we really received these truths, and do we know how completely we are loved by our heavenly Father, unconditionally?

How can we break this fear that has sought to extinguish our fire? I have good news. The kingdom of God is near. There is hope and a way back to the fullness and fire of God. God is waiting for us to come. He is waiting for all the hungry and thirsty to come to Him in repentance and faith. For me, this is summarized in Mark 1:15 when Jesus said, "The time has come … The kingdom of God has come near. Repent and believe the good news!" We break fear, or any other stronghold of the devil, through repentance and faith. This is the gateway to everything in the kingdom of God.

Turn to Jesus with all your heart and trust Him to enable you to live a new life. When we recognize our sin, repent, and turn to Jesus we can receive His mercy and forgiveness, and by His grace we can rebuke that fear, and by the authority of the name of Jesus we come against its hold on us. Then, again by grace, we ask the Holy Spirit to come and replace that fear with His perfect love so that we can be renewed and begin to live a new life in His resurrection power. This is the way back to the fire. It is about genuine repentance, faith, and fullness of the Spirit.

Quenched by Disappointments and Disobedience

Fear is not the only fire-quencher. The Bible gives us so many examples of God's own people withdrawing from Him and so sadly resisting His fire. Israel knew about encountering the fire of God. One of the most remarkable appearances of the fire of God in the Old Testament was the pillar of cloud and fire that remained in the camp of Israel in the wilderness. Here was a highly visible sign and wonder on a national scale that lasted for forty years. Just imagine walking through the camp of Israel and seeing this Presence. How could anyone ever doubt God's presence with His people?

I find it amazing that despite such a demonstration of power, the people still rebelled against the Lord. Numbers 14 is a powerful example, as the people grumbled against Moses and Aaron. This so grieved the heart of God. Reading Numbers 14 gives a fascinating insight into Moses' relationship with God and their conversations. God wanted to destroy the nation of Israel and begin again with Moses, yet Moses pleaded with God. He prayed in Numbers 14:14:

They have already heard that you, Lord, are with these people and that you, Lord, have been seen face to face, that your cloud stays over them, and that you go before them in a pillar of cloud by day and a pillar of fire by night.

In the context of the people's rebellion, Moses' appeal to God was based on His fiery presence with them, and the most visible sign of that was the pillar of cloud and fire. Here was the grace of God, that even though the people sinned, the fire was still in the camp. They were marked by the presence of God. This was Moses' appeal to God. His intercession for the rebellious people brought the mercy and grace of God, and yet there was the revelation of a limited blessing because of their disobedience. That generation would not enter the Promised Land. Yes, God would go with them, but they reaped what they had sown and so their blessing was partial.

We may think that this is very Old Testament treatment for the people, until we look into the New Testament and find that this is often how Jesus speaks to us. In John 15:1–8, Jesus emphasizes the point that it is only by remaining in Him that we can bear fruit. Look what happens when we do not remain in Him. In verse 6 Jesus says, "If you do not remain in me, you are like a branch that is thrown away and withers; such branches are picked up, thrown into the fire and burned." Also look at Jesus' words to the seven churches in Asia Minor in Revelation 2 and 3. I have read this again recently, and I always find myself a little shocked at Jesus' words in Revelation 2:5 about what will happen if they choose not to repent: He will come and remove their lampstand.

In John 15 and Revelation 2 there is a clear implication of negative consequences as faced by the people in Numbers 14. Why do I point this out? The people of Israel had seen the fire of God in the camp. They were marked by God's presence, yet they were still disobedient. Somehow, despite His grace and love, they chose to turn away from God, even while right at the centre of His manifest presence. Jesus also saw this as an issue. People who had tasted of God's presence could still refuse to repent when they grew cold spiritually.

I don't want us to make that mistake. You can be in church. You can read this book and go to conferences on revival. However, unless you and I are rightly related to God from our hearts and unless we live a repentance lifestyle of continual turning to God and remaining in Him, we will miss out. We won't enter the full inheritance that is available to us. We may wither or have our lampstand removed.

Lukewarm is not normal. Our God is a consuming fire. We were made to be like Him. Our identity in Christ and our destiny as His loved people is to burn with His passion, love, and holiness. Our assignment is to reflect His burning heart in the world. We can only get that heart from a direct connection to Him and encounter with Him. Many people are not prepared to go there. The place of encounter causes some people to grumble, and if they have cold hearts, it causes offence and sometimes people refuse to repent. They stand on their religion or their long church service record, but refuse to come to Jesus for fire.

Moses reminded God that He had been seen face to face by the people. I love Moses' appeal as an intercessor because it was based on reminding God that the relationship between God and Israel was an intimate, fiery, presence-based relationship. God responded well to that intercession. He was reminded of His fiery love for Israel. That is why I believe the cure for the church today is in a deep, intimate, radical encounter with God. This is the answer for church growth and health. It is this presence I look for in every church gathering: God remaining with us as we remain in Him; His fire burning around us as our hearts burn in Him. Not better programmes or smarter principles, but the manifest presence of God. The world needs and wants to see a church on fire, marked by God's fiery presence. We need to find healing for our disappointments and freedom to restore joyful obedience.

Moses' passion was for relationship with God, while Israel's concern was only about what God could do for them. Even back in Exodus 20, God had appeared on the mountain to give the law, but the people "remained at a distance" (Exodus 20:21). God had wanted the people to know Him face to face.

His design was relationship, but they were not interested. Only Moses really got what God was offering; the others were afraid of the fire. The fire was too challenging and frightening for them. It disturbed their sin and so the people did not go up on the mountain. What a tragedy that the people of God were afraid of the fire.

We are far from perfect. We still sin and let God down in many ways, but He remains faithful. Consider the early churches at Corinth or Galatia where there were issues of immorality and legalism. The answer is not in less fire, but more. True holiness, freedom, and love are found in encountering God as the consuming fire. We need the fire. The devil doesn't mind you seeing the fire, as long as you stay at a distance. May we choose fire.

Don't Put Out the Spirit's Fire

There is a choice. We can fan the Spirit's flames or snuff them out. I love the practical instructions in 1 Thessalonians 5 calling the church be what the church was meant to be: rejoicing always, praying continually, helping the weak, being patient, and striving to do good to everyone. In this amazing set of exhortations comes the phrase in verse 19: "Do not quench the Spirit." Some translations say, "Do not put out the Spirit's fire."

Paul is calling us not to fight the fire of God. Some people may frown on passion or display coolness rather than fervency, but we are called in God's word not to quench the Spirit. We all know the enemies of the fire of God. In 1 Thessalonians 5, I see Paul's list of powerful instructions as a fire-starting manual. Let's take a look:

> Now we ask you, brothers and sisters, to acknowledge
> those who work hard among you, who care for you
> in the Lord and who admonish you. Hold them in
> the highest regard in love because of their work. Live
> in peace with each other. And we urge you, brothers
> and sisters, warn those who are idle and disruptive,
> encourage the disheartened, help the weak, be patient
> with everyone. Make sure that nobody pays back wrong
> for wrong, but always strive to do what is good for each
> other and for everyone else.
>
> Rejoice always, pray continually, give thanks in all
> circumstances; for this is God's will for you in Christ
> Jesus.
>
> Do not quench the Spirit. Do not treat prophecies
> with contempt but test them all; hold on to what is good,
> reject every kind of evil.
>
> May God himself, the God of peace, sanctify you
> through and through. May your whole spirit, soul and
> body be kept blameless at the coming of our Lord Jesus
> Christ. The one who calls you is faithful, and he will do it.

1 Thessalonians 5:12–24

This Scripture is very challenging and encouraging. It reminds us that it is Him we need more than anything else. We need God. As verses 23 and 24 point out, this is all only possible in His strength. He is faithful in His calling us to this life of fullness and fire. In our own strength, it is impossible to live for God. But "He will do it".

Do you want to return to the Lord today and humbly call on Jesus' name to renew the fire in your heart? Are you desperate to break the chains of fear, disobedience, and distance? Are you willing to make a commitment not to run away from the fire of God? Don't wait for someone else to rise up. Now is the time for you to catch the fire again. Don't waste any more time. Get on your face before God and cry out to Him for a new day of fire in your life.

Chapter 8

White-hot Mission

As I looked,
thrones were set in place,
and the Ancient of Days took his seat.
His clothing was as white as snow;
the hair of his head was white like wool.
His throne was flaming with fire,
and its wheels were all ablaze.
A river of fire was flowing,
coming out from before him.
Thousands upon thousands attended him;
ten thousand times ten thousand stood before him.
The court was seated,
and the books were opened.

Then I continued to watch because of the boastful words the
horn was speaking. I kept looking until the beast was slain
and its body destroyed and thrown into the blazing fire. (The
other beasts had been stripped of their authority, but were
allowed to live for a period of time.)

In my vision at night I looked, and there before me was one
like a son of man, coming with the clouds of heaven. He
approached the Ancient of Days and was led into his presence.
He was given authority, glory and sovereign power; all nations
and peoples of every language worshipped him. His dominion
is an everlasting dominion that will not pass away, and his
kingdom is one that will never be destroyed.

Daniel 7:9–14

These verses in Daniel may seem like a strange place to begin thinking about a passion for mission. What does this fiery throne room scene have to do with sharing the gospel in our communities? As I have looked at what the Bible teaches about the fire of God, this Scripture really hit home to me when I realized that here in these few verses we catch a glimpse of eternity and the presence of fire in both heaven and hell. I had never seen that before. There aren't many places in the Bible that describe both types of fire within so few verses. I had only ever associated hell with fire, but God's fire is much bigger than hell, as we have seen. I love reading this description of heavenly fire.

This got me thinking more about the fire of God as a fire that reveals eternity and also our mission as a church. Let me put it simply as I can. There is fire in both heaven and hell, and I believe we are to be alight with the fire of heavenly love and compassion so that we can see people rescued from the fire of judgment. We need heaven's fire so we can save people from hell's fire and so they can share heaven's fiery love with us. It is about living life from the river of fire to rescue people from the lake of fire.

Living for Eternity

Eternity is not a trendy subject. Yet it is one of the most important issues for us to consider. Preachers used to cry out, "Where will you spend eternity?" This may be old-fashioned, but it is absolutely the right question, and one that does need a clear answer. The stakes are high.

Are we living with eternity in mind? Jesus lived in a way that had eternity very much in mind. Jesus' mission was to secure our relationship with God and our eternal home in heaven. He went to "prepare a place" for us (John 14:2–3). In fact, the whole message of salvation has to mean that Jesus came to save us from something harmful. He saves us from sin and death and brings us into eternal life. Jesus spoke about both eternal punishment and eternal life.[28] Our eternal destiny matters so much to Jesus that He gave His life for us to be saved. Jesus' sacrifice on the cross and His resurrection from the dead have opened the way for us to know God now and for all eternity.

This must make us think again about how we live our lives here on earth. The Christian life is not about us getting what we want from God; it is about us serving others and sharing our lives proclaiming and demonstrating the good news of Jesus. God wants to light a fire in us for the sake of the world. I think that captures the heart of white-hot mission. We live for others to be set free.

Are we seeing people come to Christ in our communities? We are called to so live, proclaim, and pray that we would be astonished if no one were converted to Christ. When did you last lead someone to Christ? We believe in the Great Commission, but are we obeying it?

28 For example, Matthew 25:46 and Mark 10:30, just for starters.

I long to see more people come to Christ today. The kingdom of God is designed to grow, advance, and expand. It is natural for every Christian to want everyone to know Jesus. I live in a town of nearly 40,000 people. Perhaps on a good day we have something like 5 per cent of the town as part of one of the churches. That leaves around 38,000 people untouched, disengaged, or indifferent to Jesus and His church. This makes me ache. These are precious people to God. He loves each one with such love. Every one of them can be saved and they are looking to us to show them Jesus. What do they find when they spend time with us? Are we carrying Jesus to them? Are we being the light of the world?

Churches in the UK are considered large if they have more than 400 people coming along, even on the fringe. Numbers don't impress me, but I believe we need to begin to pray with more boldness for tens and hundreds of thousands to come to Christ. I love hearing when anyone comes to the Lord, but I long to see people coming by the hundreds and thousands out of darkness into His marvellous light. As in past revivals, we long for genuine, authentic, powerful conversions of thousands of people born again with a burning heart.

This has often happened since the first revival in Acts 2. Even a quick glance through the book of Acts reveals a church on fire with mission zeal and growth. Thousands were coming to Christ, and signs and wonders were being done in Jesus' name. The Christian life is about serving and sharing Jesus with others.

Why this indifference to the lost? Do we care about people who are without Christ? I would rather speak to you about His love than His judgment. I don't want to focus on hell. I would rather give heaven the attention, but the love of God constrains us to reach out. I never want us to speak of hell without real compassion and love that breaks our hearts for people. May God save us from cold doctrine of hell that does not weep for the lost. God wants everyone to be saved through Jesus – everyone (1 Timothy 2:4).

Something powerful happens when we are set on fire with love for God. I remember it happened to me very soon after being filled with the Holy Spirit. God took away my fear of what people might think of me and gave me a passion for sharing Jesus with everyone around me. When I tasted of the fire of intimacy with God, I could not hold back. Telling others just flowed out. I didn't care what people thought any more because I knew God loved me.

Living from Heaven's River of Fire

Let's go back to the Scripture in Daniel 7:9–10. What a remarkable picture of the immediate presence of God we see in those verses. The scene of authority, purity, and awe is breathtaking. Fire is all around in the immediate presence of God. The throne of God is ablaze and a river of fire flows from that throne. In Revelation 15:2 we also read of a sea of fire in heaven. In this revelation in Daniel 7, we are privileged to access eternity and the heavenly realms. There is no more glorious place in time or eternity than the very courtroom of heaven and the throne of our Father God.

Many people are aware of the vision of the river in Ezekiel 47 that flowed from the temple to the Dead Sea. That river of fresh water has been described as the river of the Holy Spirit, and it speaks of the cleansing and healing power of the gospel. It was a river deep enough to swim in, and Ezekiel himself was encouraged to keep going deeper.

We have been talking about being on fire for God. In these verses in Daniel we see the throne of fire and the river of fire. Just as with Ezekiel's river vision, I believe we are called to get into Daniel's heavenly river of fire. I believe it is a river of cleansing, power, encounter, holiness, love, worship, joy, and righteousness. I believe this river represents the Holy Spirit, just as Ezekiel's river does. God is so glorious. We need to get into and live in the river of God's fiery love.

No wonder it was tongues of fire that came at Pentecost. Fire is a significant prophetic symbol of the Spirit. Within the Godhead, the Holy Spirit is seated on His fiery throne and His fire fills the throne room of heaven. But how can we relate to this awesome scene? God is on His throne of fire, but how does that make a difference to us? The truth is hard to really take in because it is so powerful. In Ephesians 2 we read our story of salvation, and there is a huge statement in verses 6 and 7 that changes everything for us.

As for you, you were dead in your transgressions and sins, in which you used to live when you followed the ways of this world and of the ruler of the kingdom of the air, the spirit who is now at work in those who are disobedient. All of us also lived among them at one time, gratifying the cravings of our flesh and following its desires and thoughts. Like the rest, we were by nature deserving of wrath. But because of his great love for us, God, who is rich in mercy, made us alive with Christ even when we were dead in transgressions – it is by grace you have been saved. And God raised us up with Christ and seated us with him in the heavenly realms in Christ Jesus, in order that in the coming ages he might show the incomparable riches of his grace, expressed in his kindness to us in Christ Jesus.

Ephesians 2:1–7

We were dead, wrath-deserving sinners, but because of His great love Jesus made us alive with Him; not only that, but we are seated with God in the heavenly realms so that we might put on display His glorious grace and kindness. This is where we belong: with Father, Son, and Holy Spirit in the heavenly realms. This is our true home. We are citizens of heaven and called to live from that place of His glory (Philippians 3:20). We are to set our affections on things above, not on things of earth (Colossians 3:2). This is what it means to live from heaven to earth. We don't need to fear or be led by the world, because we are not of this world. Our home is seated with Him, submitted to Him, in the fiery heavenly realms. This is where we get our fire. We spend time with Him in that place of the Word, worship, prayer, obedience, rest, and His presence. We access His fire by His grace.

This realm is where a white-hot heart of mission is moulded and stoked. That is why people who spend time with God always have a heart for mission. Anyone who knows what it is to be in God's presence will always love the lost. We cannot spend time with God and not love people. 1 John 3 and 4 make it very clear that "We love because He first loved us" (4:19). Being children of God and having His love lavished on us means that we will love others. I can't honestly think of any better way to love people than to share Jesus with them.

This is all about igniting a burning heart for mission that is urgent, fiery, rooted in love, and centred on God. Evangelism training is great, but you can't get this fire from a manual or a training day. It comes from God's heart to your heart. It comes from knowing God in the secret place. It comes through living with heaven's perspective and accessing the heavenly realms through the Bible, worship, prayer, obedience, and love. White-hot mission comes from intimacy with God.

I remember some of my early experiences at university in St Andrews as God began to fill my heart more and more with His presence. This also led to more passion for mission. This was a significant time of igniting fiery mission and a burden for the lost in my life. I remember in St Andrews seeing the letters "PH" carved into brick on the pavement in North Street. PH are the initials of Patrick Hamilton, a preacher in the early Scottish Reformation. When he was only twenty-eight years old Patrick Hamilton was burned at the stake for preaching the message of salvation by grace through faith in Scotland.

I can remember standing on that spot, praying for that passion in my own life. I spent time praying for the lost in that small town and began to gather others to pray too. Soon afterwards we started an outreach on the streets that took over every Saturday while I was at university. We could not help ourselves. We had to share the gospel with everyone, and we didn't care what anyone thought. We were not ashamed of Jesus. This was not cold duty, but love-filled obedience to Jesus' call to go and make disciples.

Something I used to do at that time was to sit on a bench in the main street and watch people. I did this for one reason: to pray that God would stir a passion for the lost in my heart. I never want to be indifferent to the eternal destiny of people who don't know Jesus Christ. I prayed and wept on that bench, just watching people shopping and milling around. They did not know Jesus and so would be lost without Him. Jesus wept over Jerusalem. The people were like sheep without a Shepherd (Matthew 9:36).

While I was a student, ignited by the fire of evangelism, God put three words on my heart that were significant for my vision to see many come to Christ and encounter His love: passion, compassion, and intercession.

Passion for Jesus

This is absolutely essential. Jesus is at the centre of mission. Without a passion for the Lord Jesus, what are we sharing with people? Let's be people who are constantly amazed by Jesus, always in touch with Jesus and obsessed by how wonderful He is. There is no one like Him. Do you love Jesus? Is He your all in all? Are you often speaking of Him? Does He fill your heart and mind? Are you continually worshipping Him?

It's time to recover your passion for the Lord Jesus Christ along with a firm conviction about who He really is. Jesus is the one and only begotten Son of God, was conceived of the Holy Spirit, and born of the Virgin Mary. He is God's Anointed King, empowered by the Holy Spirit to establish God's kingdom on earth. He was crucified for our sins, died, was buried, was resurrected, ascended into heaven, and is now alive today in the presence of God the Father and in His people. He is true God and true man. He is unique, incomparable, and matchless in grace and truth.

Jesus is so very much more than a beloved symbol of the church. He is the living Lord of the church and all creation. We are called to live with Him at the centre and in His authority.[29] He cannot be ignored or made safe. Jesus is

29 A. W. Tozer, *Gems From Tozer*, Send the Light Trust, 1969, p. 5.

radical in holiness and love. He is the answer to what it looks like to walk the earth on fire for God. As Duncan Campbell wrote, "Frequently I say that the baptism of the Holy Spirit is in its final analysis is not manifestations [*sic*], it is not gifts. The baptism of the Holy Spirit is the revelation of Jesus."[30] We need to be with Jesus and inflame our hearts with who He is, so we can be more like Him.

Compassion for People

Mission is 100 per cent love. The one absolute necessity is love. You can have everything else, but if there is no love, nothing will happen (1 Corinthians 13). Mission is not about winning arguments or pushing the gospel on people. I hate it when people are manipulated into making decisions for Jesus. That kind of fake activity does far more harm than good. Jesus never cajoled people into faith.

Let's be fiery, passionate, and wholehearted, and let that be shown through our love, sincerity, honour, and kindness as we point people to Jesus. Compassion treats people sensitively without compromising the message. We are to really listen to people, unconditionally serve people, and honestly love people. I understand that sometimes we have been fearful of offending people and have called it sensitivity. To be honest, people will always be offended by the gospel, but we are to show that gospel in the way we speak and interact with

30 Campbell, *The Price and Power of Revival*, p. 16.

people in such love, so that even if some are offended because of righteousness, they will have been treated with genuine compassion and feel cared for.

The message of the gospel has eternal implications and can seem heavy to people. It takes courage to share our faith in Jesus as the only way to God. I can't think of anything more loving than risking your own life to pull people out of a burning building. That is a great picture of mission. Remember the brave firemen of New York on 9/11: they ran into the burning buildings to rescue people with no thought of their own safety. They did that because they had made the decision long ago to risk their lives in the line of duty. I believe we need to take on a similar mindset of the church as a gospel rescue service doing whatever it takes to get people to safety in Jesus.

Compassion meets the needs of the whole person. We are to love the whole person, not just their soul. God loves them, body, soul, and spirit. Matthew 25:31–46 reminds us of the urgent importance of caring for the last, least, and lost in every way. Social action is core to the gospel. We are to love and reach people and care for them with the love of Christ. John Wesley described social action and social holiness. That is how God sees it. It is fully part of compassionate white-hot mission. We need to serve the lonely, prisoners, addicts, the poor, the hungry, and the broken. I believe God's heart is for the poor and the hopeless.

Paul had this compassion when he wrote in 2 Corinthians 5:14–15:

For Christ's love compels us, because we are convinced
that one died for all, and therefore all died. And he
died for all, that those who live should no longer live
for themselves but for him who died for them and was
raised again.

This is white-hot compassionate mission. In Romans 9:1–3
Paul wrote:

I speak the truth in Christ – I am not lying, my
conscience confirms it through the Holy Spirit – I have
great sorrow and unceasing anguish in my heart. For I
could wish that I myself were cursed and cut off from
Christ for the sake of my people, those of my own race.

Evan Roberts caught this compassion through a vision of hell
and God's judgment. In 1904 he pleaded with God to shut
hell's door for one year. Have you ever prayed a prayer like
that? In that year an estimated 100,000 people came to Christ
in Wales. There is urgency about compassion. Oh that we
might see the infinite value of a soul.

Intercession for Revival

Pentecost was born in a prayer meeting. Intercession seems
like a lost art today. I believe it is time again to offer ourselves
as learners in the school of prayer as the disciples did in Luke
11:1: "Lord, teach us to pray." We have forgotten how to ask
and plead for the promises of God's word. Remember that

God keeps His promises, and that is the work of intercession: to plead those promises afresh in our generation.

God has always had a hard time finding intercessors (Ezekiel 22:30). He is looking today for people of love and persistence to stand in the gap with bent knees, wet eyes, and tender hearts. Psalm 119:126 records how "streams of tears flow from my eyes, for your law is not obeyed". Such is the love-filled, intimate heart of an intercessor. Prayer feels deep concern for the lost who are without Christ.

Intercession is about others, not us. Maybe that is why it is such a neglected ministry. Prayer has become too often about us. We need to begin to ask for others. Intercessors are well known in heaven. It is an unglamorous ministry to the world, but glorious to God, and powerful for kingdom advance and mission fruitfulness. We are tempted to think we are insignificant, but prayer always precedes the extraordinary acts of God.

What is intercession? I believe it starts with us listening to God's heart: hearing His heartbeat and praying His word and will. The revelation of God's heart is the starting place. We cannot expect people to put their faith in Jesus as Saviour if we His people are not prepared to put our faith in Him as a prayer-answering God. I learned so much personally in prayer from Revd Dr Colin Peckham, a South African preacher and former Principal of the Faith Mission Bible College. He always spoke of the need for people who know not just how to say a prayer, but also how to pray in the power of the Holy Spirit. He emphasized intercession as laying hold of God and getting right through into His presence to find grace in time of need, refusing to give up until the answer comes.

Rescuing People from Hell's Lake of Fire

Looking again at the incredible picture in Daniel 7, we sadly see that the glorious scene of the fiery throne of God gives way in verse 11 to the terrifying lake of fire. This is the end point of the judgment of God. The evil beast was thrown into the lake of fire. Hell is not a mythical doctrine; it is a real and eternal destination. Hell is deeply disturbing to us. We don't like the idea because we cannot conceive of God using hell in His judgments, because of His goodness. These are issues of first importance for us to wrestle with. Hell should not make us rest easy.

I recently read the whole New Testament right through over a short period of time. Jesus did not mince His words. We can only understand eternity through relationship with Jesus. He spoke about eternity, heaven, and hell more than anyone else in Scripture. For example, read His teaching on the rich man and Lazarus in Luke 16:19–31. Other examples include Matthew 7:13, 19; 10:28; 13:41–43 and 25:31–46; Mark 9:48 and John 5:29. I have only chosen a few here of the many that could be selected. Jesus makes frequent reference to fire, condemnation, and eternal punishment. In fact, most of the references to the fire of God in the Bible concern the judgments of God.

I believe the Bible is very clear, very honest, and therefore very compassionate about hell.[31] Jesus wanted to warn people. Hell is a place of eternal punishment prepared by God for the devil and his fallen angels, but it is also reserved for those who have rejected Christ. In Revelation 20:14–15, hell is described as the "lake of fire" or the "second death".

The more I journey into the heavenly Father's heart of love, the more I also believe He is a God of judgment. We need to believe the whole counsel of God, not just the bits that are agreeable. God is simultaneously good, holy, loving, and just. He must punish sin and yet He saves sinners. Let's remind ourselves of the gospel. The best summary of the gospel message is in the book of Romans. I would recommend that if you feel very exercised by these things you read the entire book of Romans and then settle it with God in prayer. The Bible teaches that all have sinned. All have rejected God and are guilty and sadly are condemned. God is not willing that any should perish and He has made a way of salvation through Jesus Christ (see Romans 1–3). Only through Jesus can we be saved and come out from under the wrath of God.

I believe in heaven and hell and that believing the gospel is the only way to God. Salvation comes through Jesus Christ,

31 For further reading I would warmly recommend Francis Chan's book, *Erasing Hell*, David Cook, 2011.

and Him crucified. I would love to believe everyone will get an automatic ticket to heaven, but I don't have that luxury. If I believed that I would be making it up. The Bible says that unless we are born again, we will not see the kingdom of God. I don't want to distort the gospel by making it fit my sense of justice. We need a bigger view of God. God will do right.

If God's judgment was merely imaginary or symbolic, why did Jesus come to die on the cross for our sin? If eternity does not matter, why did Jesus speak about it so much? If we are all going to be OK, why does the Bible warn us to prepare for eternity? Why would Jesus command us to go and make disciples of all nations if it doesn't matter in the end who you worship? I would prefer hell not to be real, but what sort of justice would there be if God ignored sin?

We need to proclaim this gospel with love and truth. Let's be really clear: God does not want anyone to be in hell for one second. He wants everyone to repent and be saved (2 Peter 3:9). Salvation matters to God. Through our sin, we chose separation from God, and through His love, God chose to come down to save us. All the love is on His side towards us. We don't deserve that love, but Jesus came and now we need to receive His gift of new life for eternity. The way is open to heaven. Jesus died not only to take us to heaven, but also to bring us into eternal life now. We can be saved right now. We know God's kingdom is now and also yet to come in heaven.

The gospel is that Jesus is the only way, truth and life. No one comes to the Father except through Him (John 14:6).

The last part of the Scripture in Daniel 7:13–14 takes us back to the centrality of Jesus to the gospel:

> *In my vision at night I looked, and there before me was one like a son of man, coming with the clouds of heaven. He approached the Ancient of Days and was led into his presence. He was given authority, glory and sovereign power; all nations and peoples of every language worshipped him. His dominion is an everlasting dominion that will not pass away, and his kingdom is one that will never be destroyed.*

This vision gives us a greater revelation of the glory, goodness, and love of Jesus. When we really encounter Jesus, we won't be able to stop telling others of Him. How could we stop sharing? We come to know Jesus Christ, the One with all authority, glory, and sovereign power. Every nation will worship Him. He is the King who has eternal dominion. This King Jesus is more than glorious. How can we describe Him? There are no words fit to portray or express Him. This is the mystery of our salvation. This King is the One who calls us His friends. We get to know Him personally. There is absolutely nothing average, mundane, or routine about Him. I wish I could describe Him more adequately. Daniel saw His glory. Have you and I been totally captivated by our Saviour and Lord? Are we proclaiming and demonstrating this powerful gospel?

We Need Fiery Proclamation

Isn't it time we did justice to the glory of Jesus in the way we share, declare, speak, and preach Him? We have briefly considered the high stakes of our salvation. Jesus paid the full price for us to be forgiven, set free, and made new. This is amazing! Jesus' blood covers it all. My sin and shame are gone under the blood. Only Jesus could make us right with God. He is worth speaking, singing, and shouting about. Isn't the name of Jesus worth having on our lips? In our culture of ever more fear of proclaiming absolute truth, I believe we need to be unashamed to speak and share openly of Jesus.

Do people know about Jesus from meeting us? Do our lives and words speak plainly of Jesus? Does what we say about Jesus match how we live with Jesus? It's not OK to be ashamed of Jesus. We have had enough bland preaching and faith sharing with no conviction or substance. People in the world are not interested in a dreary or pale Jesus. They are looking for the real Jesus we read about in the Bible, and He has given us the job of representing Him to them. We don't need to use a megaphone or shout on street corners, but I am asking us to consider the passion of the message we have. Let's share Jesus in our offices, schools, hospitals, homes, buses, training, supermarkets, gyms, and restaurants – everywhere.

Paul said he was "not ashamed of the gospel, because it is the power of God that brings salvation to everyone who believes: first to the Jew, then to the Gentile" (Romans 1:16).

Jeremiah knew the same experience. In Jeremiah 5:14 God says to him, "I will make my words in your mouth a fire." Again in Jeremiah 23:29 God says, "Is not my word like fire?" Whether we preach or share in a small group or in one-to-one conversation, what matters is the fire and passion, courage and clarity; the love and compassion with which we openly share Jesus. I would love every Christian to have a testimony of leading others to Jesus.

We Need Fiery Demonstration

Alongside proclamation of Jesus, and no less important, we need to let there be a demonstration of Jesus and His kingdom for all to see. Paul made this very clear in 1 Corinthians 2:1–5:

> *And so it was with me, brothers and sisters. When I came to you, I did not come with eloquence or human wisdom as I proclaimed to you the testimony about God. For I resolved to know nothing while I was with you except Jesus Christ and him crucified. I came to you in weakness with great fear and trembling. My message and my preaching were not with wise and persuasive words, but with a demonstration of the Spirit's power, so that your faith might not rest on human wisdom, but on God's power.*

We need a demonstration of the Spirit's power today. It is time to see signs and wonders, miracles, and healings, and also to see justice flow like rivers. I believe evangelism, signs and wonders, and justice are bound up in the gospel demonstration. This gospel heals the sick and brings freedom to the oppressed.

The church was always designed to destroy the kingdom of darkness. In the Great Commission, we received power and authority over sickness, sin, and the devil. Our assignment is to seek first and advance the kingdom through bringing freedom to captives, healing the sick, delivering people from the demonic realm, and promoting justice and righteousness. Some people think this is impossible. How could we do these things? My answer is very simple: "Christ in you, the hope of glory" (Colossians 1:27). It is God who works in us to His glory. The gospel is to be demonstrated supernaturally by us in the power of the Spirit. This is mission through Word and Spirit.

We have seen this demonstration time and again on our streets as we have prayed for people outside the church who have been healed, helped, or even come to Christ for the first time. We love taking opportunities as a church family to reach out, whether through Family Fun Days, Street Pastors, Foodbank, Healing on the Streets or Café Hope. We always seek to demonstrate the gospel with signs and wonders and love as well as proclaiming Jesus. We want to see the sick healed, the oppressed set free, and the hungry fed. There is no greater joy than leading someone to Jesus. Everyone can lead someone to Christ. This calls us to alter our lives. Stop living only for time, but for eternity.

Here is a Scripture that has kept me awake at night. It is very challenging, and at its heart is the call to live out the gospel and demonstrate Jesus:

> *"Not everyone who says to me, 'Lord, Lord,' will enter the kingdom of heaven, but only the one who does the will of my Father who is in heaven. Many will say to me on that day, 'Lord, Lord, did we not prophesy in your name and in your name drive out demons and in your name perform many miracles?' Then I will tell them plainly, 'I never knew you. Away from me, you evildoers!'"*

> Matthew 7:21–25

Speaking about these verses, Francis Chan said the word that makes us most nervous is the word "many".[32] Many of us can talk a good talk, but are we living it out? Do we live as though we really know God? There is a similar teaching in Matthew 25:31–46. These are some of the most convicting verses in the Bible. May we live out the gospel in word and action. Remember, there is no condemnation for those who are in Christ Jesus, but here's the thing: make sure you are in Christ Jesus. Paul writes in 2 Corinthians 13:5, "Examine yourselves to see whether you are in the faith; test yourselves. Do you not realize that Christ Jesus is in you – unless, of course, you fail the test?" The ones who are safe here are those who are

32 Chan, *Erasing Hell*, pp. 118–119.

being who God wants them to be, sharing, proclaiming, and demonstrating the gospel – on fire for God! Salvation is not by works, but we want to make sure we are actually following what Jesus said. We don't want to live anywhere near the borderline. Let's be those who live out the gospel with our words and deeds.

Jesus paid the ultimate price not just to get me from hell to heaven, but also to put heaven inside me, so that every day I could defeat the powers of darkness. The fire of God is revealed in white-hot mission. Don't you burn to lead others to Him?

Chapter 9

It's Time for Burning Hearts

"Were not our hearts burning within us while he talked with us on the road and opened the Scriptures to us?"

Luke 24:32

D
o you have a burning heart? My heart burns within me when I read the Scriptures and God speaks to me. My heart burns when I share my faith with someone in need. I burn as I lift up my hands in worship and simply become aware of His presence. I believe the burning heart is essential for every Christian. As we have been discovering the many manifestations of the fire of God, doesn't your heart burn within you for more of Him and more of His fiery presence? I believe it is time for our hearts to burn with God's fire.

In the amazing story of the road to Emmaus, we find two men who were devastated because they felt they had missed out on what they thought God was going to do through Jesus. You can read the whole story in Luke 24:13–34. We meet them as they were walking home. They were deeply disappointed, depressed, and confused. They had even heard rumours of His resurrection, but were still defeated in their hearts.

Jesus described them as "slow to believe". As He broke bread with them, "their eyes were opened and they recognized him". Their hearts burned as Jesus spoke with them and opened the Scriptures to them. I often feel very much like these men on the road. I am too slow to believe, just as they were. I have heard the rumours of fire from heaven as I read God's Word and see Him moving in the church, and yet I remain slow to believe. I think the experience of these men on that road is very close to what many of us feel today. We long to believe and see great things. We long to be part of the advancing kingdom of God. Like them, we can feel perplexed, let down, and disillusioned. Much has been promised, but all we have seen has been failure. We have heard the wonderful prophecies but seen little change. Our hopes were raised, but came to nothing.

Then Jesus came to them and everything changed. He opened the Scriptures to them. He shared His heart with them and they were in relationship with Him. They encountered Jesus and never recovered. They described the experience as having burning hearts. How we need Jesus to come to us by the Holy Spirit. We need to see the Scriptures with His eyes of fire. We need Him to share His heart with us so we can be in relationship with Him. We need to encounter God so our hearts would burn with His fire. Are we living in this encounter?

Just as every Bible character did, you and I desperately need the fire of God. I am hungry for the reality of His holy fire in my life. I want my life to be marked by Him. To read about the fire of God is one thing, but to obtain and experience it ourselves is another. Wesley Duewel writes:

> *God has created our spirits flammable. We are spiritually combustible. Our nature is created to be set ablaze by the Spirit. We are spiritually most blessed, most victorious, most usable when we are ablaze. We are most Godlike when we glow with holy flame – the flame of the indwelling Spirit.*[33]

For years we have fireproofed our lives with our idols, busyness, possessions, agendas, and selfishness. We struggle to seek something we have never experienced before, but the truth is that God is able to transform our lives with His fire.

I believe it is time for fire. Govan Stewart wrote, "When the fire of God falls on a human life it comes with consuming power, purifying, possessing and radiating light and warmth in the midst of darkness."[34] Many believers don't realize what God has made available. I want you to be filled with the hope and promise that you can be filled with fire by God's grace. You and I need never be disappointed in God. His fire is as powerful today as ever. You can receive the fullness of God and His fire burning in your heart. Are you satisfied with what

33 Wesley L. Duewel, "The Holy Spirit will Set You Ablaze". Available at www.heraldofhiscoming.com/Past%20Issues/1997/January/the_holy_spirit_will_set_you_ablaze.htm (accessed 21 July 2015).
34 I. R. Govan Stewart, *When the Fire Fell*, The Faith Mission, Edinburgh, 1961, p. 6.

you are becoming? Have you begun to call out for the fire to make the difference and change you on the inside?

So where do we begin? The answer is simple, but extremely challenging. We must be completely honest with God about our spiritual condition. Have I a vision of my own cold heart and desperate need for God? Have I settled for something less than God intended for me in my Christian experience? Unless I can see the need for a spiritual revolution in my own heart, I will not find the fire.

It's About Him, Not Me

This is where it starts, this inner place of honesty, humility, and holy desperation. We start at the end of ourselves. This is why the breakthrough on the Emmaus road was so powerful. The transformation was not based on the men, but on Jesus. He had burned in them.

This is a vital lesson for every Jesus follower. It is not about us; it is about Jesus. We have no rights. We are His disciples first and foremost. We have been giving precedence to self-preservation rather than spiritual passion. Our greatest enemy is selfishness and the desire to hold on to our opinions, agendas, offences, excuses, and strongholds. That is why fire is the answer. It burns up every trace of sin and releases the light and glory of God into our lives.

Have we understood that all this is not about us? We are not at the centre. We aren't to live from what we just feel like doing. His truth and His Word are to dominate our experience. We are to be full-time for Jesus.

I believe we will never be on fire for God until we come to the place of intimacy with God and full surrender. The people I meet who are most full of the Spirit and most joyful are not at all self-centred. The fire has burned up that stronghold and they are free to live for God in the power of the Spirit. We see this selfless life in Revelation 12:11, where we read that they overcame the devil through the blood of the Lamb and the word of their testimony, and that "they did not love their lives so much as to shrink from death". We see it again in Philippians 3:10: "I want to know Christ – yes, to know the power of his resurrection and participation in his sufferings, becoming like him in his death." We would all say we want to know Christ and experience His power, but are we willing to become selfless, humble, and powerless, and to participate in His sufferings? The way to up is down in the kingdom. We humble ourselves and God lifts us up.

What does it mean to deny self and hold nothing back? Here are a few more Scriptures to pray over and to challenge our mindsets of comfort, ease, and selfishness:

Therefore, I urge you, brothers and sisters, in view of God's mercy, to offer your bodies as a living sacrifice, holy and pleasing to God – this is your true and proper worship. Do not conform to the pattern of this world, but be transformed by the renewing of your mind. Then

you will be able to test and approve what God's will is –
his good, pleasing and perfect will.

Romans 12:1–2

Then he called the crowd to him along with his disciples
and said: "Whoever wants to be my disciple must deny
themselves and take up their cross and follow me."

Mark 8:34

Then he said to them all: "Whoever wants to be my
disciple must deny themselves and take up their cross
daily and follow me."

Luke 9:23

For to me, to live is Christ and to die is gain.

Philippians 1:21

I have been crucified with Christ and I no longer live,
but Christ lives in me. The life I now live in the body, I
live by faith in the Son of God, who loved me and gave
himself for me.

Galatians 2:20

This is the first step in freedom. Lay everything down and
surrender. You have got to let Him have you. It's time to bow,
to be bent lower still at His feet. This is not about servitude,
but passionate love. The gospel is full-on surrender. This is
why I believe the Western church struggles so much. We are
battling with surrender, hoping for an exemption or a shortcut.
There lies the reason for our powerlessness. This issue of the

Lordship of Jesus needs to be settled in our hearts. Living out His Lordship brings freedom from the tyranny of self. Aren't you tired of living without His fire?

Freedom and Fire: Knowing Our Identity in Christ

Only when we deny self, as Jesus and Paul both taught, can we discover our real identity in God. We have to be free from our old self so we can put on the new self, created to be like Jesus (Ephesians 4:24; Colossians 3:10). So many Christians are living in fear, which is rooted in self-centredness, and so they still experience captivity rather than fire and freedom.

I believe freedom is vital to a life on fire for God, and this freedom comes not through church programmes but through the finished work of the cross. Freedom comes through Jesus Christ, and Him crucified (1 Corinthians 2:2). Finding the freedom to live on fire for God starts with the simplicity and power of the gospel. In his letter to the Corinthians, Paul was concerned that they were drifting away from the pure gospel and that this would hinder their discipleship. In 2 Corinthians 11:2–3, he writes:

> *I am jealous for you with a godly jealousy. I promised you to one husband, to Christ, so that I might present you as a pure virgin to him. But I am afraid that just as Eve was deceived by the snake's cunning, your minds may somehow be led astray from your sincere and pure devotion to Christ.*

In other words, Jesus Christ is all you need.

For such a long time I heard superb teaching on knowing your identity in Christ, and to be honest I foolishly ignored it. It didn't seem to touch me. I could not really understand its relevance to my life. It all seemed a bit too indulgent to focus on my identity. How wrong I was!

Over the past few years I have become convinced that fully knowing who God has made us to be is absolute dynamite and essential for living in the power of the Holy Spirit. Knowing who God is and who He has made us to be is incredibly powerful in helping us be free from self and to live for the kingdom. It promotes intimacy, security, fellowship, honour, and worship. We need to stop living with victim mindsets and excuses, thinking from the old self. We must not put our identity in ministry, but in our royal relationship with God.

Know who you are as a son or daughter of God and let everything flow from that identity. The first step is in freedom from the old self, but then put on your redeemed and righteous identity in Christ and be empowered in that identity. In our salvation, Jesus has restored the glory that was lost to humanity through the Fall. Paul writes powerfully about this adoption to sonship that so changes our identity to live as children of God:

For those who are led by the Spirit of God are the
children of God. The Spirit you received does not make
you slaves, so that you live in fear again; rather, the Spirit

you received brought about your adoption to sonship.
And by him we cry, "Abba, Father." The Spirit himself
testifies with our spirit that we are God's children. Now if
we are children, then we are heirs – heirs of God and co-
heirs with Christ, if indeed we share in his sufferings in
order that we may also share in his glory.

I consider that our present sufferings are not worth
comparing with the glory that will be revealed in us. For
the creation waits in eager expectation for the children
of God to be revealed.

Romans 8:14–19

This glorious identity is a gift from God. Walking in this identity empowers us to rejoice through sufferings, because we know they are not worth comparing to the glory that will be revealed. Can you see that when we embrace this gospel gift of freedom, we can be empowered to be filled with the fire, and no matter what happens, we will live for God's glory, not our own? We have died to the old way of life and have been raised to live a new life – a life of fullness and fire (Romans 6:1–14).

Throughout much of this book, I have sought to be faithful in relating and sharing the standards of the kingdom and the radical teaching of Jesus. I don't want to lower the standard of God's Word to our lack of experience. But I know that this radical lifestyle of fiery discipleship makes many feel condemned because they feel powerless to live it out. My dear friend, there is zero condemnation, shame, and guilt for those who are in Christ Jesus.

How can we defeat this fear and condemnation? I believe the answer is in sincerely and humbly knowing myself as a beloved child of God, knowing and living from the kingdom identity Jesus died to give to me. What God says about us is all that matters. We don't compare or consider what others think of us. I need to grasp the depths and security of being unconditionally loved by my Father in heaven, who loved me even when I was His enemy, before I knew Christ. If He loved me when I was a lost, sinful, hell-deserving unbeliever, then how much more, as I am now His child, will He freely give me all things (Romans 8:32)? Remember, unless we change and become like little children, we will not even enter the kingdom (Matthew 18:3).

So as those men on the road to Emmaus were burning in their hearts because they met Jesus, may the fire fall on us as we meet with Jesus in worship, prayer, prophecy, and the Bible through the power of the Spirit. He speaks to us! Isn't that amazing? May God's fire increase in us because we are in living relationship with Him. We have access to God through the blood of Jesus. Fire comes from relationship with God. It really is that simple.

Set Me on Fire

Jesus died and rose again so you could have a God-filled personality. It is perilous to cool off spiritually. We are to be spiritually flammable. I believe God wants to move in our generation in an unprecedented way. He is looking for a fiery people who are willing to count the cost, to go through with God, to be filled with the fire of the Spirit, and to advance the kingdom of God. We need to get alone with God, to grow in intimacy, and to fan the flame.

The Greek word for "fan into flame" in 2 Timothy 1:6 refers to the use of a bellows to cause a smouldering fire to flame up. This takes effort. Timothy was to do everything in his power to intensify the manifestation of the flame of the Spirit. Our cooperation with the Spirit is essential to consistency of flowing ardour, spiritual radiance, and flaming zeal. That fanning must be a continuous process. Five times in Leviticus 6 God instructed that the fire on the altar of burnt offering was never to go out. He had sent that fire from heaven (Leviticus 9:24; 2 Chronicles 7:1). God supplies the fire, but we must make every effort to keep it burning.

When we pray to be set on fire, we are asking the Lord for His presence; for revival; for refining, power, holiness; and most of all that we might love well. Spiritual fire requires spiritual fuel and oxygen to burn. This is what I believe it means to be set on fire for God. A fiery Christian will look something like this:

- Believe God's Word and listen to His voice.
- Be hungry to pray, worship, give, and witness.
- Know the Father's love and their identity in Him.
- Submit to Jesus and take up their cross daily.
- Be filled and dependent on the Holy Spirit.
- Sacrificially love and serve people, especially the poor.
- Keep the gospel simple and central.

I passionately believe that God wants to raise up a fiery church today. He is calling out an army of ordinary, extraordinary fire-starters. Samuel Chadwick wrote many years ago:

> *Wesley, Whitefield, and General Booth wrought wonders by the Fire kindled of the Holy Ghost. Men ablaze are invincible. Hell trembles when men kindle. Sin, worldliness, unbelief and hell are proof against everything but fire. The Church is powerless without the fire of the Holy Ghost. Destitute of fire, nothing else counts; possessing fire, nothing else really matters. The one vital need is fire. How we may receive it, where we may find it, by what means we may retain it, are the most vital and urgent questions of our time. One thing we know: it comes only with the presence of the Spirit of God, Himself the Spirit of Fire. God alone can send the fire. It is His Pentecostal gift.*[35]

35 Chadwick, *The Way to Pentecost*, p. 96.

So What Are We Waiting for?

"Lord, set us on fire. We ask that our hearts may burn within us. May we never be the same again. Do such a deep work of grace in our hearts. Burn in us with holiness. Ignite us with courage to never be ashamed of Jesus. Take over, Lord Jesus. Teach us to pray, to deny self, and to depend wholly on the Spirit. We don't ask that it may be easy, but we do ask that we may see this and every nation experience the manifest power and presence of God in revival fire. Father, we come honestly and humbly. Set me on fire, Lord. Set us on fire, that Jesus may be glorified. In His beautiful name, Amen."

May you ever burn brightly for His glory.